OLUREMI VICTORIA AYIDA

Her Life & Ministry

D1740960

Jewel of God

by

Mosope Macarthy-Chiadika

Foreword
by
Pastor Enoch A. Adeboye

FRIENDSHIP BIBLE FELLOWSHIP MINISTRY
(NIGERIA) BOOKS

© Mosope Macarthy-Chiadika 2007
Jewel of God

ISBN: 978-0-9555648-0-2

Published by:
Friendship Bible Fellowship Ministry (Nigeria) Books
15 Grove End Road
London
NW8 9SD

In Nigeria, this book can be obtained from:
Helen Baugh House
96 St. Finbarrs College Road,
Akoka, Lagos, Nigeria
Tel: +234(01) 774 74 29

E-mail: fbfm@hyperia.com
sopemac_chiadika@yahoo.co.uk

A CIP catalogue record of this book
can be obtained from the British Library.

Designed by:
The Better Book Company Ltd
Forum House
Stirling Road
Chichester
West Sussex
PO19 7DN

Printed in England

OLUREMI VICTORIA AYIDA

Her Life & Ministry

Jewel of God

by

MOSOPE MACARTHY-CHIADIKA

DEDICATION

Dedicated to the
Glory and Honour of the Almighty God –
The Blessed Trinity
Who alone authors and helps man to accomplish purpose
and
All members of Friendship Bible Coffees (Nigeria).

"One of the jewels in God's timepiece of redemption." – Selwyn Hughes

FOREWORD

The core values of Mrs Oluremi Ayida are summed in the opening paragraph of Chapter 2 of this book: Honesty, humility, loyalty, generosity, commitment and faithfulness. They have served her well. Very well. From the humble beginnings in Edo State and her adolescent years in Lagos, these traits have advanced the person and ministry of Mrs Ayida to the very top of not just her career but in the international community as well. With these values she has always been wired by God for special assignments.

When I had the special privilege of first meeting her about two decades ago, these core values were well developed. I have had the additional blessing of seeing them flourish. An avid reader of *The Word*, she is the prime mover of the introduction and distribution of the widely acclaimed devotional *Everyday with Jesus* in Nigeria. Through her determination, the devotional has spread all over the country. Denominational boundaries are no barrier to this wonderful woman of God. Her relationships endure and she is often a rallying point. This in part is responsible for the success and growth of the "Friendship Bible Coffee Fellowship" in Nigeria. This fellowship has continued to attract the affluent housewives who invariably bring their husbands in.

This biography of a most extraordinary and remarkable woman of God chronicles the walk and call of the Almighty with Oluremi Ayida through the journey of a lifetime.

It is a treasure trove for anyone interested in a close walk with God and who wants to fulfil his destiny and life purpose. I strongly recommend this book to every Christian pilgrim.

Pastor E.A. Adeboye
General Overseer,
The Redeemed Christian Church of God

ACKNOWLEDGEMENTS

I appreciate the several people who made this landmark book a reality. May the Lord bless you all richly for your immeasurable support.

The Allison Ayida family, for sharing your lives and experiences in order that lives be touched and changed for God's glory. You have enhanced in no small measure the richness and tangibility of this book. May God make your house a perpetual blessing.

My subject herself, Oluremi Victoria Ayida, this book owes its existence to the large amount of information you have supplied over the many months of work. Your simplicity and sincerity in sharing your story unreservedly is rooted in the depth of your personal convictions, commitment and service to God and humanity through His Son Jesus Christ and empowered by His eternal Spirit. You have preserved and passed to future generations, the testimony of God's faithfulness – how He has helped you fulfil His purposes on Earth.

Pastor (Dr) Mrs Grace O. Macarthy, my mother and first Christian influence.

Daddy, Pastor E.A. Adeboye, for your fatherly care and exemplary life of selfless service to the Kingdom of our Lord Jesus Christ. I am specially thankful for your esteemed support and invaluable contribution to this book.

The late Reverend Selwyn Hughes, for his prayer and invaluable contribution to this book.

All men and women of God that have contributed variously to this book: your prayers and support, your resource materials and comments that have been made use of. May God's Words in your mouth continue to be true. May lives continue to be established and prosper, as they believe in God and His prophets.

To all FBFM staff and FBC members in Nigeria whose faith, support and warmth continue to encourage many lives in no small measure; keep fanning the fire and the flag flying!

My brother, Pelumi Macarthy, for your time to drive me down for most of the interview sessions I had.

Kayode Akinwale, for your encouragement in writing this book.

Pastor Femi Mosaku – Johnson, for your editorial assistance and advice for this book.

Everyone who took out time to oblige me of their personal impressions of Mrs Oluremi Ayida. You have spoken not as sycophants but in truth of your convictions. Thank you for believing in the work. You are all a delight!

Femi Ogunsan, for your time to work together in the initial proof reading.

Mrs Alero Ola, through whom I joined the FBC fellowship over six years ago. May your godly spirit continue to draw many more to the place of their fulfilment in God.

Bensol Printers (Nigeria) Ltd. For handling all the initial typing.

Angela Salomon for the invaluable time we had having a final review and for doing all the final typing of the manuscript. Thank you for being an encouragement.

My editor, Jill Field, and her team at the Better Book Company.

My husband and children, your constant love and support in diverse ways cannot be over-emphasised. Thank God for making you His joy!

Above all, to the Infinite Person – the Holy Spirit: my life, my inspiration, wisdom and strength.

TABLE OF CONTENTS

Then those who feared the LORD spoke to one another,
And the LORD listened and heard them;
So a book of remembrance was written before Him for those who
fear the LORD
And who meditate on His name.
"They shall be Mine," says the LORD of hosts,
*"On the day that I make them **My Jewels.***
And I will spare them as a man spares his own son who serves him."

Malachi 3: 16 – 17

INTRODUCTION

'A prophetic book'

On the 25th November 2003 the title *Jewel of God* was impressed on my heart by the Holy Spirit. As I pondered, it became explicitly clear that it was the book title of the biography of the life and ministry of Oluremi Victoria Ayida, which I was being privileged to write. Almost immediately I pulled out a pen and a white sheet of paper and began to jot down the contents page as though it was being downloaded into my mind at that point in time. I quietly tucked away the paper into my work file where it was for another two months as I occasionally thought of what the project involved: the fact that I was presently busy with another writing project and the aspect of gathering materials for the work. Some weeks into the New Year after I had sought counsel, I decided to start work on the biography project.

Armed with tools of the detective, the details of the novelist, as well as the patience and compassion of a priest I commenced the first meeting with Oluremi Ayida on the 11th March 2004. It was at this meeting she told me she had prayed some time ago of her desire to leave a written history of her life but she did not exactly know how this would be. An affable woman, assiduous, with spiritual prowess I had always closely observed her in the many fellowship meetings and outreaches we had had as a ministry over the years. Here I was now one-to-one with her – it is this personal relationship and experience with Oluremi Ayida, her family and ministry that makes *Jewel of God* real, vivid and deeply personal and suffice to say an answer to prayer!

An intriguing story, *Jewel of God* is about a life full of God, faithfulness, excitement and a great example worthy of emulation. *Jewel of God* is an exposition of the mind of God to inspiring, motivating, correcting and advancing His people towards reality, practicality, responsibility, purpose and destiny. The *Jewel of God* is a sixteen chapter prose book of uniform content style that endeavours to have a glimpse of God's work sent from eternity into time by the inspiration of His Spirit to His Praise and Glory. It is a well of discoveries with lessons of wisdom available to anyone who would choose to look closely. In drawing parallels and receiving instruction, it is noteworthy to say that no two lives will ever be exactly the same! There is uniqueness to ou: walk through life that will not be duplicated elsewhere. Emphasis is laid on understanding principles and values, obtaining guidelines and receiving truth by God's word. The entire book reveals the statement: **"I AM WHAT I AM BY HIS GRACE"** (1 Corinthians 15:10) as it unfolds three major facts of this truth. The fact of purpose – everyone God creates, He equips with talents, giftings, spiritual grace (treasures), friendship (relationships) to fulfil one's purpose in life. The fact of the new creation through God's Son given to the world and the fact of one's living faith. My heartfelt prayer is that God will use this book to positively impart and impact you into finding and fulfilling your God-given purpose and destiny in this lifetime to God's glory and to also encourage you in your faith and in your walk with Him. Remember you are a unique person destined to make an individual unique impact!

'Sope Macarthy-Chiadika
February, 2007

OLUREMI VICTORIA AYIDA

Her Life & Ministry

Jewel of God

by

MOSOPE MACARTHY-CHIADIKA

1

HER PERSON

The Spirit of God has made me,
And the breath of the Almighty gives me life.
Job 33: 4

For you formed my inward parts;
You covered me in my mother's womb.
I will praise you,
For I am fearfully and wonderfully made.
Psalm 139: 13 - 14

Oluremi Victoria Ayida was born to her father, Mr Misilaw Cheke, an Itsekiri from Ugbodede; a descendant of the House of Iteye of Warri Kingdom, Delta State in Nigeria; and her mother, Madam Ajiwun Sabalemotu Dosunmu of the Dosunmu Family of Itagarawu, Isale Eko, Lagos state.

Of her parents, she recalls:

"My father was an only child of his mother, and he was pampered. Both the father and the mother petted him. As a result of being an only child, when he grew up, he was allowed to have as many wives as he could lay his hands on. I grew up with my mother and she happened to be a Muslim, but despite the fact that I was living in a Muslim environment I decided to go the Christian way. So from the age of five I was going to church. She encouraged me. At times, she wanted me to go to Quaranic School, which I did during the week and then on Sundays, I attended Church."

Her father had ten children, but her mother had just her and her sister, Mrs Esther Nanna, for their father. They both grew up under their maternal grandmother in Siluko town, Edo State where Oluremi was born. Her grandmother cared for them a lot, even though Remi yearned to be with her father. When her father eventually left Siluko for Lagos, not having gone with any of his wives, Oluremi left and joined him in Lagos. She recalls her father then was dealing in "Abura" (he was a timber merchant) and was working with an expatriate, Mr Joe Brandler. She stayed with her father for sometime and went to elementary school. After a while, she decided to move into a family set-up which brought her to start living with a cousin, Mr Obuku Awani at Badley Avenue, in Yaba (now Herbert Macauley Street). He had three wives and one of them took responsibility to foster her, her sibling and some other relatives.

However, she recalled that her mother was responsible for her school fees from the proceeds that came from her trading and business activities and she often paid them visits bringing foodstuff for the family to show her appreciation.

Oluremi Ayida's primary school days started in 1937 at Ladilak School where she was till 1942, before leaving for Reagan Memorial Baptist School, also a primary school. She recalls the particular incident that motivated her switch over to Reagan Memorial. "The Baptist Missionaries came for a Revival programme held at Ladilak School. It was at that service that I received the baptism of the Holy Spirit and spoke in tongues. I was very small. I didn't know what I said or anything else, but the missionaries were joyous over me. They visited me regularly at home, nurturing me and inviting me for bible studies. As a matter of fact, I had a Holy Ghost experience at an early age in my life."

She adds: "After this, I moved to the Reagan Memorial Baptist School at Sabo, Yaba because Ladilak was more of a secular school. They had morning devotion but not like that of the Baptist and Methodist schools."

Her classmates at Reagan amongst others were Mr Tunde Johnson and the late Mr Femi Johnson, the senior brothers to General Mobolaji Johnson, (a former military Governor of Lagos State and one of the most successful Governors of the military era). She spoke of the children that attended the missionary schools then as quite different, in that they were refined and cultured because of the effect the missionaries had on them.

In 1944, Oluremi took the Common Entrance Examination. She gained admission to the famous Methodist Girls' High School then at Broad Street, Lagos. Shortly before the Schools' New Year started in January, the Methodist Girls' High School was moved to Yaba and many other secondary schools were also moved to the Mainland of the city to make way for the military personnel accommodation. The

Methodist Girls' High School was then moved back to its original site at Broad Street on the Island between 1945 and 1946.

Oluremi was there till she took her School Certificate Examination in 1950. She made the choice to study Nursing, so, immediately after her secondary school, she went straight to the Lagos General Hospital, took the qualifying exam and gained admission in 1950. On what attracted and motivated her into the Nursing profession, she puts it this way. "Firstly I hate to see people suffering, I empathise with the sick. The Red Cross of Nigeria Association headquarters was next door to our house at Makoko. I used to go there to see them and watch the first aid training and I decided to join the Association from my school days. It was from this connection with the junior Red Cross Association that I decided to go into the nursing profession. Secondly, my mother was struggling and working so hard to educate my sister and me; and I could not bear to see her working so hard, so I decided to start my nursing career, where the trainee nurses were paid. I wanted my mother to take a break from all she had done in the past."

After a year of studying Nursing at the hospital, she got a sponsorship from her father's partner, Mr Brandler, to travel abroad to pursue her nursing career. Oluremi Ayida continued her Nursing dream and travelled to the United Kingdom in 1951 where she studied three years of general Nursing at the Bishop Stortford Hospital, Hertfordshire, obtaining her State Registered Nurse Certificate (SRN) where she also worked briefly. In 1955, she went to North Middlesex Hospital for the first part in Midwifery training and afterwards to Thorpe Combe Hospital, London for the second part. The second part of the Midwifery course called "the District Nursing" gave licence to a midwife to deliver women in their homes. By 1955, she was through with her training. In 1956, she took the Public Health Course, for one academic year at the Battersea College of Technology, now The University of Surrey, Guildford under the sponsorship of Kent County Council. She worked for the council for one year as a Health Visitor and School Nurse and had the job of running child welfare clinics, by seeing to the welfare of babies, toddlers and school children. At the end of her one year obligatory service to the Kent Council she decided to return home to Nigeria in December 1957. She joined the Western Region Ministry of Health in 1958 and was posted to Ijebu Province as the Health Visitor in Health Centres and

District Midwifery. Her work involved travelling to the remote areas in the Ijebu Province. Her area covered Ijebu – Ode, Remo, Epe, and Lekki Peninsula Divisions. According to Oluremi, "I used to go by motor boats from Epe to Lekki because then there were no land routes. I was stationed at Ijebu – Ode and travelled daily except on weekends. I enjoyed my work very much, helping the less privileged and they were very appreciative. The Western Region Government gave wonderful and comprehensive medical services to its peoples in those years …" On her career Oluremi continued narrating,

"Whilst I was working for the state government my husband was working as a civil servant for the Federal Government of Nigeria. I had to seek employment in the Western Region, because back then, a policy of not employing married women in the Federal Public Service was in place. Later on, the politicians fought for the abolishment of this law. At this time my husband was in charge of the budget in the Ministry of Finance, and seeing that in the department for the Ministry of Health there were vacancies for Health Sisters, I was asked to apply. I went for an interview and because of my experience of working in the rural areas, I was offered one of the positions which I took up. However I was not satisfied with working for the Federal Government because they were in charge of hospitals and not preventive medicine. I decided to apply to the Lagos City Council which was responsible for Public Health Nursing, it was here that I made my mark." In recognition of her service and experience Oluremi Ayida was seconded from the Lagos City Council to Lagos State to establish one of the Health Centres in the State. Among the three Health Sisters chosen was also Mrs Omowunmi Akinsete who became a close associate and friend of Mrs Ayida in the Public Health Service. Mrs Akinsete established the Health Centre on Lagos Island whilst Mrs Ayida established the one on the Mainland at Randle Avenue in Surulere. Oluremi stated that she succeeded at this because she had all the necessary support from the Chief Nursing Officer and the staff of the Lagos State Ministry of Health. To enhance her work, the then Medical Officer of the Public Health Service, Lagos City Council, the late Dr Tunji Adeniyi-Jones, who was also her boss and who also seconded her to Lagos State, recommended that she should go to England to train as a Public Health Administrator. In 1967 she went for the course at William Rathbone Public Health Nurse College in Liverpool. She coins it, "This training has helped me tremendously in my interacting and understanding of human relationships. I give the glory to God. I can see now that God was preparing me, for the service in His Vineyard."

Oluremi was involved with the Professional Association of Trained Nurses of Nigeria (PATNON) and the Nurses' Union of Nigeria. The former being a member body with an International affiliation for Nurses who trained overseas. She was very much involved in this and became the National Treasurer with the duty of opening and operating bank accounts amongst other duties for the Association. She remained the treasurer for over eight years. The latter was the National Trade Union of Nigerian Nurses. Mrs Ayida was a committee member of this Union which presented the Nurses' case at the Udoji salary review panel in 1974. Through the PATNON, Oluremi attended international Nurses' conferences in Tokyo and Canada, which were held once in four years. Mrs Ayida was also made an Honorary member of the Public Health Association of Nigeria.

She was also actively involved with Family Planning training and became a member of the Family Planning Society of Nigeria. Through this she was sponsored to visit other countries. One of the sponsorships she recalled was through the World Bank. The World Bank sponsored and organised quite a number of projects through Ford Foundation and USAID Programmes on family planning. The first work was a USAID sponsored project in 1968, where she travelled in the company of a Ghanaian Health Nurse to Nairobi, Pakistan, Taiwan, Turkey and Egypt. Through the Ford foundation programme, Oluremi travelled with some of her colleagues namely Mrs Akinsete, Mrs Anu Adegoroye, Mrs Shogbola and two others, to America and the Caribbean in 1972. This trip was facilitated by a privileged opportunity Oluremi had when she travelled earlier with her husband to America. Recounting, she puts it, "In my life I never allow any good opportunity to pass my way without seizing it and making good use of it. One of those opportunities was when I accompanied my husband to the Commonwealth Finance Ministers meeting in the Bahamas and the World Bank Meeting in Washington DC. It was during this meeting that Mrs Carter, wife of the former U.S. President, Jimmy Carter invited wives attending the meeting with their husbands to a tea party at the White House. It was an honour and a privilege that I would never forget. It was there that the wife of the World Bank President, Mrs McNamara (who had previously been to Nigeria with her husband, and my husband and I had hosted a party in their honour) asked me if I would like to come on an observation visit of field work in family planning in the Caribbean and in Harlem, New York City. I accepted the invitation on the condition that the offer could be extended to some other colleagues. To my amazement she agreed. Mrs McNamara then got the Ford Foundation to sponsor the trip for about six nurses in Nigeria. My nominees amongst others included Mrs Akinsete and Mrs Shogbola, who are now my sisters in the Lord and co-ordinators of the Friendship Bible Coffees Ministry." Oluremi Ayida was awarded an International USAID Certificate of Achievement in the field of Family Planning in July 1972.

Conclusively, Oluremi Ayida remarked that God had prepared her and endowed her with such Administrative skills that anywhere she goes, she is always made to organise, plan and co-ordinate; a job she is still very much interested in and involved with presently. In her Nursing Career, she served voluntarily as the Chairman of Lagos City Council Branch of Public Health Nurses of Nigeria. Also as a council member of the Federal Nigeria Society for the Blind from 1978 to 2000 and as a voluntary worker for the Nigerian Girl Guides Vocational Centre for Handicapped girls, Lagos from 1984-1987. Also as a member of Girl Guides of Nigeria and leader of the Ikoyi Brownie Pack.

Oluremi Ayida retired from her Nursing Career in 1976 from the Lagos City Council Public Health Service as a Senior Health Nursing Officer. She was given an Honorary award of the Fellow of West African College of Nursing. (FWACN) on the 18th March 1997. The honorary fellowship was awarded for distinguished services and worthy contribution to Nursing and humanity.

If man is not made for God, why is he only happy in God?
Blaise Pascal

2

HER PRINCIPLES

Woe to you, scribes and Pharisees, hypocrites! For you pay tithes of mint and anise and cummin, and have neglected the weightier matters of the law: justice and mercy and faith. These you ought to have done without leaving the others undone.
Matthew 23:23

For though by this time
You ought to be teachers,
You need someone to teach you again
the first principles of the oracles of God ...
Hebrews 5: 12

Honesty, humility, loyalty, sympathy, generosity, commitment and faithfulness have been the underlying principles, intrinsic values upon which Oluremi Ayida has built on unto maturity and stability by the grace of God through the years. These principles have formed the basis of her relationship both vertically (with God the Creator) and horizontally (with fellow human beings). Not only does she work with these principles but appreciates to see them in the lives of people she relates with. She states that when she gives someone an appointment, she expects it to be kept. If for any reason, the other party is unable to make the appointment she appreciates a prior notice either by phone or whichever way to cancel it rather than not hearing from the person. She reveals that for some people you would not even hear from them at all on or before that day's appointment and perhaps even for the next three months or even at all. Mrs Ayida describes such people who break an appointment or cannot keep their word as unreliable. "I like committed people," she remarks. From her school days to her career years and beyond, that quality of commitment has been in her.

It is this quality that attracts and favours her selection for leadership positions in various associations she has been involved with over the years. She expresses, "I like to associate with committed, honest and faithful people. I cannot stand anyone who is proud. I love people who are humble."

Oluremi affirms that these principles have built her up even when she was not a Christian. Recalling instances of her empathic and sympathetic nature, Oluremi Ayida is easily moved by the suffering of people. As a former Nurse and Health officer, she could not watch a child die, she would cry. She is moved when she sees anyone suffering, she empathises with that person.

During her career years whilst lecturing trainee nurses she would counsel them, that whenever they see a patient, depending on the age of that person, they should think:

"This could be my mother or father, brother or sister, aunt or uncle or even my own child." Once that thought is established in them, they are moved to attending to that person with a committed, empathic heart. She said that has been her motto: "putting myself in another person's position."

Talking about her loyalty, which spans from her school days, she recalls her friendly relationship with Mrs Madarikan (Nee Craig) who was the senior prefect of the school while she was in form four. It was a case of someone in lower class being the best friend with her senior. They got so close that they often wore the same dresses for occasions. Even when she could not afford it, her best friend's mother would buy them for her. When Miss Craig was getting married, Miss Oluremi Cheke was her Chief Bridesmaid. She expresses that she likes making friends with people even older than her. Asked her reason for this choice of friendship, she remarks that there is so much to learn from them and that God favours her by giving her people who always gives her a helping hand.

She also recalled that when she started her Nursing Career in the U.K, the Staff Nurse who was in charge of her ward became her best friend. "She would not eat without seeing me. God has given me this gift to build healthy relationships and to be a confidante. You see an older person crying on me, and I'm telling them something to comfort and encourage them. I am loyal to the few friends that I have;" this is the way she succinctly describes her friendships.

Many of Oluremi Ayida's principles have been translated into action. They have formed the underlying foundation of her life, which has a direct bearing on her attitude to the essence of life generally, more so now being built on the foundation of Christ. As Mrs Esther Arinola Nanna, Oluremi Ayida's sister says, "She is very kind, loving, generous and motherly ... who can go to any length to help those who are in need."

Mrs Comfort Omatsone, a very close family friend of over thirty eight years confirms, "Mrs Ayida, as one that readily from the depth of her heart, empathises with people who are in one difficulty or another; and is ever willing to offer Godly counsel and where necessary, offer practical assistance."

Her attitude to God

"I fear God," remarks Oluremi Ayida describing her attitude to God. She further said that the fear she meant is not a "shaking fear", one born of coercion from a taskmaster or forceful ruler. Rather it is the fear of His Love, His Greatness, His Omnipotence, Omnipresence and Omniscience. Simply she says, "In my heart I do fear God. I long to grow more Godly with each passing day. I call the fear of God being in awe of Him and scared of any sin that would mar my life and separate me from His Love." The encounter she had with God as a young school girl though memorable was "lost" along the line. As she grew up "mixing with the world", she said "she lost touch with God". She only remembered Him when in trouble or when a relationship was broken. Mrs Oluremi Ayida likes doing things for the Lord. Enthusiastically she volunteers as the need arises to clean the church, to visit someone, or make transportation available, for a cause or something which is in her God given ability to do. "I love doing things for the Lord, and not just me alone, I involve my family, my children." How does she do this? She narrated giving an instance. Anytime she is travelling to Stonecroft Ministry, in Kansas City, USA for Christian seminars or conferences with other delegates from Nigeria; she informs her son there and he helps to look for the most reasonable flight fare from New York to Kansas City. He arranges the booking for the benefit of everyone travelling from Nigeria. Her sister's children in New Jersey also help to accommodate some delegates in their house during such trips. She concluded on this that when you are involved in a good cause, your children would emulate you.

Speaking about her expectations from people in response to her zeal in being of help to others, Oluremi says God has taught her to look to Him for reward. Paraphrasing from the Bible in Hebrews chapter eleven the sixth verse, she remarked that the arm of flesh has failed her several times. She says rather than feeling disappointed, she sees and experiences God as a rewarder. Oluremi Ayida describes God as the Faithful One who never fails.

As a spinster, she made some requests born out of her personal desires to God. She prayed to God for a husband without a mother. The reason for this being that she had heard so many stories about mothers-in-law. She prayed also to have four children, two boys and two girls. Lastly, she also asked God for a big and beautiful house with a swimming pool. Excitingly, she exclaimed that He did just exactly that and beyond. She said she met her husband, who being an only child was well cared for and pampered. In spite of all that, "My mother-in-law was of excellent help to me. All I had to do was to become pregnant and give birth to the baby, my mother-in-law would then help me to look after the child whilst I went back to work. But if God had listened to my request, how would I have coped with looking after the children and working? So He knows what is good for us. What is good, He answers it and what is not good, He brings it out," she humorously enthused.

"Your attitude to God will determine your response to His word, which in turn determine the kind of results you command." – Dr David Oyedepo.

Her attitude to the Word of God

Oluremi Ayida's attitude to the Word of God is that the Word of God is true. It is His Promise and He doesn't fail. Explaining further, she says, "The Word of God is also the key to knowing God and His will for my life. The Word of God changes my attitude to the things of this world. It enables me to focus on Christ. The Word of God is His Power for Salvation. The Word of God is my spiritual food that makes me grow and changes my life for good. It is essential that a Christian should be rooted in the Word of God, just like a plant with its roots hidden underground." She continued interestingly, "When we are secluded and alone with God, reading and studying His word and drawing from Him all that we need to live an abundant life (John 10:10); a life pleasing to Him, a life that makes a difference in our

10

communities, then we can be the people that God desires us to be. This is the aim and objective of the Friendship Bible Coffee (FBC) studies. It was through this studying of God's Word, that I gave my life to Him. Since then my first desire is the things of God. To be a woman close to God's heart. I have developed the habit of drawing near to God by routine and regular exposure to His Word, to draw out the nutrition needed to grow a heart of faith. I have learned however that my good intentions don't go very far, but by His Grace I make a conscious effort to have devotional time. The effort is worth it, because the Word of God is treasure and is fathomless. His word stands as His counsel forever. The joy of being counselled by God daily is wonderful. By His Word, I was born again (1 Peter 1:23) and by it I am growing (1 Peter 2:2) and by it I walk through life as the Word lights my path (Psalm 119:105). Therefore knowing His Word is of utmost importance to me. I discovered joy and peace in it and I grow to love Him more than anything else in this world. I have given Him the first place in my heart and He is my priority if I have to make a choice," she concluded.

Her attitude to life

In describing her attitude to life, Oluremi Ayida coins it with the five-letter word of G-R-A-C-E. She says, the grace of God is revealed in life and it is not for her to use for herself alone. It is to share her life with others. It is to be an example of what God will want her to be to other people. A life that others will see and want to serve the Lord she's serving. This has been the attitude that guides her in whatever she does. What people will think of God if she behaves un-gloriously, doing something that does not honour the Lord? Being a leader by example and a follower of Christ is the underlying consideration of her attitude to life. A life driven by God's purpose and a life that draws others to Christ.

She continues, "So my obligation because of this grace is that whatever I do must honour the Lord, it must be to His glory. Life is all about glorifying God. He hasn't given us life just to advertise ourselves or for people to sing our praise. He has given us life so that we can use it for Him. Our hand to be His hands, our eyes to see what He wants us to see and to reflect it to others. Whatever He has given us, let it be used to His glory; that has been my attitude, whatever God has given me, to spread it."

She promptly remembered however to add the temptation that Satan brings to her mind to counter the flow of God's grace in her and through her to others. With much seriousness in her tone as if revealing someone in hiding, she tells how the enemy tries to discourage her from giving generously. "Somebody gave you a thousand naira, out of this, you've spent almost 80% on God's work, why don't you allow others to..." she says, putting her words to frame the temptation.

"But I derive joy in giving, sharing my life," she concludes with a light countenance and a tone of accomplishment that comes from freedom in Christ.

Being a leader in many capacities, through the years, Oluremi Ayida reveals that a leader must not just say, "follow me". A leader must do what he wants the followers to do. A leader does not sit back and say, "do this, do that". A leader who is not responsible, she says, cannot make a leader that will hand over effectively because there is no example to follow. A leader leads by serving and by example she concludes.

Life is a privilege, not an imprisonment. You did not play any role to exist. God says "Before I formed thee in the belly, I knew thee..." (Jeremiah 1:5). Life is a gift, Life is all about:

Contributions, not Collection
Responsibility not Dependence
Relevance not Significance
Service not Status
Sacrifice not Surplus
Giving not just receiving
Disposition not Position.

Responsibility is the price for greatness. How relevant are you to people, your family members and the society? You maximise your existence by service. Life is a gift wrapped with responsibility. If you refuse to accept responsibility, you die as a liability.

Dr David Oyedepo

Her attitude to work

It is work that determines worth. Your work today determines where you sit tomorrow (Proverbs 22:29). It is your commitment to work that determines your attainment in the world. Work is the all time cure for lack and penury. It is the gateway to all round fortune and most effective physical fitness device.

Dr David Oyedepo

Oluremi Ayida's attitude to work can be described in this way. The first step is that she sets a goal and then conscientiously she works towards it. When God gives her a vision and as she begins to understand it, she then starts to work to achieving it and invariably, God always sees her through. She further explains that one cannot work towards a goal doing nothing. After praying, one has to take steps towards it, "That is the only way you can achieve your goal," she adds.

Using the Friendship Bible Fellowship Ministries (FBFM), she relates the issue of growth at inception in the Ministry as a ready example. There was a desire and a need to grow. The vision to promote the Word of God. The desire and goal to bring many to the knowledge of God through reading the bible, the tools being the FBC study classes and *Every Day With Jesus* (EDWJ) devotional. The next step taken was in the place of prayers to God, opening more homes for bible studies and inviting friends and neighbours to the study. The next step was to search for distributors for *Every Day With Jesus* (EDWJ) publication. There were specific or certain areas to be reached as well as many other places where God opens a door. At every opportunity, proper follow-up was made and a good incentive was given to motivate the distributors.

This necessitated her having to travel to different parts of Nigeria to seek openings for the distribution of the devotionals. She lays emphasis on 'hard work'. She equally advised that one should ask God what to do, having the vision, with Him being involved at every stage of the work, being focused, pursing the mission and with His help, one will reach the goal.

Still speaking in this light, Oluremi Ayida revealed that she had a weak point. She says when God gives her a vision, she first sees it as too big for her. Satan comes and puts fear in her mind. The whisper comes from within, telling her she can't do it and somehow she begins to think that way and almost concluding that she cannot do it. However, with a word of prayer from her heart to God, He always sends someone her way to encourage her, saying, "You can do it." Once she sees someone God brings to affirm the possibility of implementing the vision, she runs with it! She says even when the person is not helping in the work, she goes on with it until the goal is achieved; "And that has been the instance of everything we have done," she remarked.

Narrating how she came to Nigeria with four copies of EDWJ, she explained that almost immediately the Ministry requested a thousand copies from the author, Rev. Selwyn Hughes in England, he made that amount available adding that if the Ministry could distribute 10,000 copies within two years, he would come to Nigeria for the first time. She said they thought it was impossible. However with prayer and hard work, in less than two years, the distribution got to 10,000. This achievement which Mrs Ayida was quick to attribute to God, brought Selwyn Hughes to Nigeria. Through the Nigerian media and travelling to some parts of Nigeria, God opened the door and the distribution doubled. She continued, "I have discovered that when God is your partner, the stress is removed, favour is given, coupled with faith and action."

This attitude has been Oluremi Ayida's mode of work, not only in the Christian Ministry but also during her years as a career woman. Whenever she has an opportunity to serve, she likes involving people to join her.

She recalled that whenever there was a travelling award for her in the Nursing profession, for example on family planning work, she would readily mention at least three other colleagues extending the invitation to join her for the training programme, which they all benefited from and were able to train others as well.

Giving another instance, whenever she gets an invitation from StoneCroft Ministries, she involves other members and together they would make the trip. Conclusively, she says, "This has been my pattern, so that when I'm not there, there are others who have had that experience to carry on the work."

Humorously but firmly, I shared the scripture in Isaiah 32:8 with her as it was laid in my heart at that point. We were both encouraged and affirmed to the life of the Word once again. It was already 4.30pm on a Thursday in her office. She requested we call it a day, as she had to go home and get enough rest for a night vigil. I obliged her.

Character, more than charisma forms and sustains service to God and man.

Oluremi Ayida's life has not only contributed, but has also touched and challenged many to better and higher heights in service to God and humanity.

It is not your aptitude,
but your attitude that determines your altitude.
Zig Ziglar

3

HER PRINCE

He who finds a wife finds a good thing,
And obtains favour from the LORD.
Proverbs 18:22

For this reason a man shall
Leave his father and mother
and be joined to his wife, and
The two shall become one flesh.
Ephesians 5:31

It's always so interesting to hear love stories; how it all started between two people of the opposite sex, "love at first sight" they say! How they got along, dating, writing love notes or poems, gifts, those long walks, adding worth and appreciation to each other, getting into the higher attitude of courtship, asking questions in their hearts: could this really be true? Is this for real? Do I really love him enough to m-a-r-r-y him? – And within a space of time, the wedding bells are ringing. For Allison and Oluremi Ayida: "They both lived happily ever after!" could sum up this chapter of their wonderful love story.

It was another bright sunny Thursday afternoon in her office. Both of us were ready for the business of the day. Warmly welcomed, I took my seat across her and said, "Ma, we're having an interesting session, we're talking about your Prince, your heart-throb today!" She beamed at this. The door opened almost immediately and drinks were brought in. She was served. I declined the offer of a soft drink as I was already filled with the excitement of the day's work. Vera, one of the staff, left the office with the tray and closed the door gently behind her.

After a sip from her glass, Oluremi Ayida in her usual humble but lively and apt manner gave her first remark to the statement I had earlier made.

"Thank God," she said at first then taking a long breath in between trying to recall the events of the past, she swiftly added, "I met my husband in London ..." At this point, I knew we had both embarked on an exploration of an exciting journey to the 'love world' of Allison and Oluremi Ayida. I was all ears; my pen was set for its usual task while my little recorder couldn't wait to take in every detail of the moment. It was a long but delightful day.

Allison Ayida's esteemed contribution to this 'story' gave it the completeness needed, enhancing its richness and tangibility. And like he puts it, he shares, "We are together in this venture, amen."

How it all began

It was in 1955 at a Christmas party at 25, Almeida Road, London N.1, home of the late W.W. Fregene. A friend of hers had invited her and told her she wanted her to be at the party. She recalled that it was a wonderful party where she danced and also met some old friends and people she had never met before. At that time she was at Battersea College of Technology as a student of Public Health training. The next day, she got a phone call from "someone" that was also at the party the previous day.

Surprisingly, she asked how he got her number. He told her he had memorised it while she was giving it to someone else at the party. There was an outburst of laughter from both of us at this. Apparently, according to Allison Ayida, "She left a refrain, which I sounded all night. It was love at first sight. This love has lasted a lifetime."

He asked her out for dinner to which she obliged. She was living then at 17, Lexham Garden, London SW7. He came over to see her. Their first date was a dinner in his flat prepared by himself and a cousin, Frank Ogbemi. When she came, she took over the cooking and serving. Along the line, she discovered that he was from the same town as her father. He happened to be Itsekiri, what a coincidence, she recalled. Moreover he was born in Gbelebu, a fishing village next to Siluko town, where she was born. "His father and my father were friends, his mother and my mother were friends, he schooled at King's College in Lagos and I went to Methodist Girls' in Lagos but we never met," she recalled. Knowing that their parents knew one another gave their meeting a click. He had just graduated from Oxford University and he was studying for his Master's degree at the London School of Economics (LSE).

Courtship

They had started 'something'. Was it worth their while? They knew they wanted a relationship together and so they gave it all they possibly could. It was new; so much to know about each other that made the love to glow. It was beautiful!

Asked at what point did he have the conviction that she was the right woman for him, Allison Ayida convincingly puts it this way: "From the moment we had the first waltz: *I'll Be Loving You Eternally*, I knew she was the woman I wanted."

The news of his father's death set in motion some train of events at this time. In August 1957, he got the news, which he said made him "Very, very, sad. The only person whose approval I would seek was no more. I decided to seek her hand in marriage," he recounted.

Before then, Oluremi had written a letter to her father in Nigeria telling him of her relationship with Allison. Her father replied and said he would like his cousin, the late Chief Festus Okotie-Eboh to meet the young man. When Chief Okotie-Eboh travelled to London, he called her and asked Oluremi to invite Allison to see him. The trio had a pleasant time at a Chinese restaurant. At the dinner, her elder cousin and Allison got on very well discussing politics and at the end, he gave his consent to the union on behalf of her father. On returning to Nigeria, he told her father of his delight in the couple. In two weeks, the wedding was arranged, as Allison had to travel to Nigeria to be there for the family.

Her Happy Day

September 27, 1957 will always remain a special date to be remembered by Allison and Oluremi. In less than a week Allison, had completed every arrangement for the wedding. When he told her that they were getting married, she asked, "Where will the money come from?" He told her he had gone to book the registry and paid the money. Recounting, Oluremi Ayida said her fiancé told her he would wear his old suit but that he needed a pair of new shoes. As a Health Visitor then, she was working and earning some money, from which she bought him a pair of shoes.

She had earlier bought an outfit for herself for her friend, Lanre Fisher's wedding. Her wedding now came up, probably faster than she thought. She decided to use the outfit for her wedding.

Mr Frank Ogbemi was the best man and his girlfriend, Miss Grace Edukugho (now Mrs Ogbemi) who was a law student then in England and Remi's good friend, who had also invited her to the party where it all began, was her chief bridesmaid.

Dr Dayo Akinrele, a friend of the couple, who was at Cambridge had an old jalopy car he used in travelling from Cambridge to London. He offered to have the privilege of chauffeuring the 'about-to-wed' couple in his jalopy. Halfway to the Kensington Registry, the car packed up. Outbursts of laughter from both of us filled the air in her office. Still in laughter, she humorously continued. The 'couple' had to alight from the car and took a taxi to the registry leaving Dayo to take care of his car. After the wedding, they took a black cab to the reception. Along the line Dayo had repaired his car. The wedding reception took place in Allison's flat organised by his cousins Frank Ogbemi, Dr E. A. Ikomi and Oluremi's roommate, a lady from Ghana, Miss Helen Lamptey. The wedding reception was made up of less than twelve guests. The couple then took an overnight bus from London to Edinburgh, Scotland for their honeymoon. It was in a friend's house, who was one of his classmates at King's College, Lagos, now, Oba (Dr) K.A.O. Sansi, the Obelu of Esure, Ijebu Province. At that time he was studying in Scotland as a veterinary Doctor. On their arrival at his flat, the first thing she did was to clean up the house and wash up many used plates that had filled the sink over some time. "So for my honeymoon, I was busy cooking for two men," she added, laughing.

Life with Allison – A new home

After about two weeks of their honeymoon, Allison left for Nigeria. On arriving in Lagos, he went to see his wife's cousin, the late Chief Okotie-Eboh who was then the Minister of Finance. He was directed to meet the then Head of Service. He was employed two days later and was posted to the Ministry of Education.

While her husband was already in Nigeria, Oluremi Ayida had to still work for sometime with Kent County Council in England, having obtained a sponsorship from them. At the end of the required one year of working, she resigned and joined her husband in Nigeria in December 1957.

"I came back from England just before Christmas, I had a wonderful reception," she narrated. The ship stopped mid-sea waiting for a boat to pilot it through. However before the pilot boat could come, another boat had arrived with a delegation of customs officials and led by her cousin, the late Chief Festus Okotie-Eboh. She got into the boat amidst a pomp welcome. "It was a red-carpet reception for the princess!" I humorously added. On getting to the dock, the first place of call was at the church. She was driven to St. Jude's Anglican Church at Ebute-Metta, her church of many years before she left Nigeria. People were already there waiting for her arrival. That was the custom then in those days. It was a happy reunion with her husband as they had a thanksgiving service.

He had not yet been given accommodation at work then, but his cousin, Mr Nuke Ogbemi who was with the Ministry of Labour gave them one of his boy's quarters. It was cleared and the couple started living there in Ikoyi. She adds concerning Mr Ogbemi, that he was the same cousin her husband lived with at Campos Square area in Lagos Island when he was still at King's College as a student. It was his younger brother, Frank Ogbemi that was his best man at their wedding.

Speaking on the challenges they had as a young couple, and how they pulled through, Oluremi Ayida recalls that, financially, they had a lot of challenges. On her arrival from England, she could not take up any employment with the civil service. There was a rule in place that barred married women from gaining employment in the Federal Service. Coupled with that, she was also expecting their first child. She states, "But with the free accommodation, we were able to live on Allison's income and his cousin, Mr Ogbemi was feeding us."

"Sometimes I used to go to my father, with the little he had to ask for money," she added. Her husband she recalled, had to take up a part-time lecturing work for extramural classes for those seeking admission into university to augment his income. The classes were always held at Methodist Boys' High School, Broad Street, Lagos. However, after the birth of their first child, she got a job in the Western Region as a Health Sister for Ijebu districts. She took over from Mrs Adegoroye who was leaving the country with her husband consequent upon an overseas posting from the Foreign Service Ministry. Mrs Adegoroye later became a member of the Friendship Bible Coffees as a result of the relationship with Mrs Ayida and she is currently a co-ordinator with the ministry.

Mr Allison Ayida worked for a year at the Ministry of Education initially. The Permanent Secretary then, Mr R. M. Elphick was his tutor at King's College and with his help Allison was given an official accommodation at Ikoyi. Allison was posted to the Ministry of Finance, where he began to have a series of promotions over the years. After the Nigerian civil war, the Ministry of Economic Development was established by the Federal Government and he was posted there as the acting Permanent Secretary. He had a glowing career and made a great impact to the nurture and emergence of an endearing civil service structure in Nigeria. He reached the peak of his career in the civil service when he served meritoriously as Head of Service and Secretary to the Federal Government of Nigeria working with four Nigerian Heads of State from 1963 to 1977, when he retired.

On some of the roles his wife played in enhancing his impact and helping out in several challenges he had encountered in his career and business, Mr Allison Ayida succinctly describes her as always been a supportive woman. "She is very prayerful, she has been an anchor and has provided the bed on which I rest during the trying days. Whatever I accomplished, we did together."

The heart of her husband doth safely trust in her, so that he shall have no need of spoil. She will do him good and not evil all the days of her life.

Proverbs 31:11-12

He recounted: "When I started work as an Assistant Secretary on a salary of £624 per annum, she was earning more as a Health Sister. We learnt to live on our joint income. She can draw on my account. We pull together and have lived happily ever after. We have put our trust in God and the Lord has provided for our needs. Whatever challenges we encountered, Mummy anchors her pillar on the Almighty Lord. She prays her way through," he spoke candidly. "We operate a joint account and we still do till today," Oluremi generously added.

Graciously stating the true nature of his princess, Allison Ayida says, "She is an angel and towers above all. Her personality shines above all. She is a gem, a rare gem. Her humble bearing speaks for itself. She is ever ready to learn from her mistakes. She does not suffer fools."

On their thirtieth wedding anniversary, the marriage was solemnised with a church blessing at the All Souls' Church, Langham Place, London W.1. It was celebrated with a one week Mediterranean cruise that started from Venice.

Oluremi Ayida no doubt, has been a godly woman who has helped provide a trusting framework on which her husband has been able to share his innermost person, so that together, they have matured and reached their full potential.

In a humorous way, I asked Mr Allison Ayida if he is given another opportunity by God to have a wife afresh, would he still choose Oluremi Victoria Ayida as his better half, bone of his bones, flesh of his flesh, his helpmate, lover, confidante, best friend, mother of his children ...

With depth of conviction, he answered affirmingly, "Yes, of course!"

Many waters cannot quench
this little spark which the Lord hath kindled,
neither shall the floods of persecution drown it.
Charles Wesley

4

HER POSTERITY

Your wife shall be like a fruitful vine
In the very heart of your house,
Your children like olive plants
All around your table.
Yes, may you see your children's children.
Psalm 128: 3, 6
That our sons may be as plants
Grown up in their youth;
That our daughters may be as pillars
Sculptured in palace style.
Psalm 144:12

The thrills of Motherhood

Arrival of the first

Describing her thrills of motherhood, Oluremi Ayida said they had their first child in 1958. It was a new experience. She said "I could hardly take my eyes off her in the cot."

Speaking of her maternity, she related, "Alero was born at the Creek Hospital. Coincidentally the wife of my husband's tutor at Kings College Doctor (Mrs) Elphick was in charge of my antenatal care. A hardworking and diligent nurse took delivery of her at birth, this was Miss Sodeinde, who is now married to Professor Adesola, a renowned surgeon."

Allison Ayida affirms this, saying, "When I became a father on June first 1958, Alero brought blessings to our life." Oluremi recounted that of all her husband's friends, they were the first to get married and become parents too! So when they had Alero, their first daughter, she was showered with so much love, care and pamper from their friends. Mr Ayida recalled that they had a small party then with many of their friends: Chief Philip Asiodu, Frank Ogbemi, Dr E. A. Ikomi, Mr & Mrs Tayo Ogunsulire amongst others, whom they had stayed with through thick and thin.

Oluremi humorously added that some of their friends gave Alero nicknames such as 'Hogan Bassey', as she loved watching and mimicking the popular boxer on television. "We had much fun then, going to parties with close friends or going to listen to Victor Olaiya's music, a popular high life musician of those days," Oluremi said.

Particular event of note while nurturing the children

Oluremi Ayida recounted that it was hard for her husband to be working in Lagos, while she worked in Ijebu-Ode in the south-western part of Nigeria. Every Friday, immediately after work, her husband would drive to Ijebu Ode and be with his family till Sunday evening before returning to Lagos. She was there with their first child as well as her mother-in-law. When she went to work, her mother-in-law whom she described as a lovely and caring woman, took care of Alero. For well over a year, she was in Ijebu Ode. Through a friend of hers, Mrs Oshin, who was working at the University College Hospital (UCH, Ibadan), she got a nanny, a widow – an aunt to her friend to help her mother-in-law, in taking care of her baby and the house chores. Together, they all came back to Lagos. The nanny, an Ijebu woman, was called "Mama Muyi" but her daughter as a baby calls her "Mama yi". Everybody began then to call the nanny "Mama yi." Narrating, Mrs Ayida recalled "The woman loved Alero so much so that when she started growing up, Alero spoke with an Ijebu accent!"

Oluremi added that anytime the nanny did something wrong, she would tell her that she was sacking her, Mama yi would then quickly go and pick up Alero. When Oluremi called her daughter, Alero would not come because she was so used to being taken care of by Mama yi.

Oluremi Ayida recalled that the nanny nursed three of her children for her before she left. Despite the fact that she left, she did not go with her young son Jamiu, whom she had brought with her to stay with the Ayida's. He stayed with them for some time.

Mrs Ayida used her experience on family planning when having her own children. She said, "God granted me grace to space my children in a way that rearing them was stress free." She mentioned that their second daughter, Gbubemi was also born at the Creek Hospital, Marina Lagos. "I had another hardworking, dedicated staff nurse, Mrs Rose Disu who attended to me. We later became friends and she became a member of the FBC before going to be with the Lord."

Challenges and excitements of parenting

Speaking on the challenges and excitements of parenting, Oluremi Ayida said when all the children had now come, they gave all that they had to them. Before they thought of anything for themselves as parents, they thought of the children first. She puts it this way; "Our aim and objective was to give all our children a broad based education that would give them an advantage in life. We wanted them to have good knowledge of their country as well as other parts of the world. We encouraged them to work hard at their studies and always rewarded them for good work."

During his many official overseas tours, she said her husband always bought things for the children, but hardly bought anything for himself. She added that she was like that too. The money they had was used for their children. She went further, saying she had made up her mind that she wanted her children to go to the best schools in Nigeria, to get the best of education. She said they kept on that focus and achieved their goal.

Indeed the children attended some of the best schools in the country at that time for their nursery, primary and secondary education: Corona Nursery and Primary School, Queens College, Kings College. They also attended coaching lessons and extra curriculum activities such as piano lessons and ballet, Girl Guides and sports. "I made sure that they didn't lack anything." Speaking with a tone of excitement and motherly joy, she made reference to one Sunday morning when she woke up to see their daughter, Alero, featured in the front page of the national Daily Times Newspaper as a ballerina. This gave her some sense of fulfilment. Describing this time of their lives, she recounted that her husband was always very busy in the office, either preparing the budgets or writing speeches for the Minister or making official trips. Mrs Oluremi Ayida concluded in saying, "Though I was also working, I was there for the children." Still speaking on the children, she said they always gained admission to schools on merit. She made sure they worked up to the Advanced

(A) level before getting into the University. She continued, "Alero did her A Levels here in Nigeria then sat for the Common Entrance into Oxford University, England. When the result came out, it was excellent. Gbubemi, her younger sister was starting lower sixth, and we didn't want Alero to be alone in England, so we decided that her sister should go with her and study her A levels while Alero started at the University. All the children had their university education in England."

I asked her how the children were brought up as I thought silently on the proverb: "Train up a child in the way he should go: and when he is old, he will not depart from it."

She replied with an air of certainty, "By the grace of God, they were brought up well. God really helped us to bring them up. We took them to church to hear God's word; I was not a committed Christian at that time. They were not forward. When we had visitors, you wouldn't see them jumping around shouting or disturbing. Unless the person(s) visiting brought their own children along, then they would come and play with the children." She continued with a stronger tone in her voice, "I brought them up not to be flippant and not to retaliate. Whenever someone comes to report on my child, it's my child I would scold. I never sided with my child whilst speaking about it in the presence of the aggrieved party. After they had gone, I would comfort my child saying softly to them, 'It's all right, it's all right.' I remembered an incident," she continued after a short pause of recalling it in her memory. "I took Alero and her sister to my seamstress. As we finished and got into the car, they said, 'I want to go *wee-wee*.' The lady took them and when they came back to the car, I asked them, 'Did you go?' They said, 'Mummy, we couldn't do it, the place was too dirty,' though they didn't tell the lady that. They had been taught cleanliness," she remarked.

Concluding on this aspect of her children's upbringing she said they imbibed good morals. "Whosoever was working with us, the steward or the nanny, they were part of the family, my children would call them Miss or Mister, they would never call them cook or nanny." I listened quietly, my eyes gazing at her as she reminisced.

Treasured Times of the family

Knowing that birthday celebrations are fun moments for children everywhere, I asked Oluremi Ayida whether they had fun for their

26

children on their birthdays? "We celebrated the children's first birthdays, we always had a party for the children and one for the grown-ups too," she said.

The children were often taken on holidays and picnics where they had really nice times. Whatever their parents had was kept just to give the children fun. They visited places like Lome in West Africa, Paris, Disney World in America, Spain, Italy, Venice and Portugal. "So with what we had, we use to educate and enlighten our children in every facet of life," says Mrs Ayida.

She led me into an eventful, colourful and treasured day in the Allison and Oluremi Ayida family. It was in 1982 when their daughter, Alero, was given out in Holy wedlock. The excitement, enthusiasm, joy and fulfilment that accorded that day was still as new as it was over twenty years ago as she recounted it! I observed her golden tone with which she described the event. She narrated, "I've never seen anything like that, it was a grand wedding! It was grand because of the support and love shown to us by family members and friends." I gave a burst of applause! "Congratulations!" My mouth agape ... broadest of smiles revealing my teeth as I shared the joy of it with her. She continued interestingly: "People we didn't remember to invite were there. Even up till now, some still accuse me of not inviting them to Alero's wedding." Happy parents I thought, as I asked her how fulfilled they felt as parents that day. She adds, "On that day, when she was leaving, her father was crying, Alero was also crying. They stayed at the Federal Palace Hotel for the night because their flight to Rio was the following day. After they left for the hotel," she went on, "... we found her vanity case, and we were so happy, we took the bag, and ran to the hotel," she continued as we both laughed. "We had an opportunity to see our daughter again, so we sat down there for another twenty minutes before leaving them."

It was not only the bride's parents and siblings that missed her so much when she got married and left home. Some very close family friends whom they had all come a long way together couldn't hide their feelings also. She said, "Some were humorously asking, 'who is taking Alero?'" I prompted, "Who is the blessed man that took her?" "Dr Otobo ..." she replied. Continuing, "... Now a Professor, they met at Oxford, he was doing his PhD then," she concluded.

Look at the way Solomon puts it in the last chapter of his proverbs.

She looketh well to the ways of her household, and eateth not the bread of idleness. Her children arise up; and call her blessed.

The bulk of domestic responsibilities, it is said, lies more on the woman of the home. It is multi-faceted: physical, emotional, spiritual, financial, material, mental, social, moral to say the least. She has all duties to fulfil first to her maker, God, to her husband, her children, her extended family, her environment and herself. What a privilege, but an awesome duty! Only by the grace of God can this be accomplished.

Every wise woman buildeth her house: but the foolish plucketh it down with her hands.

Proverbs 14:21

There are many building materials required in this task. It seems Solomon, King of Israel at that time and the wisest man that ever lived, has a lot revealed on this. Probably because he had a lot of women to deal with, wives as well as concubines. He would have seen their different, individual characters, attitudes, morals, spirituality, beauty and brains. I don't even think he knew all of their personalities intimately, as there were so many of them! However, he was in a good position to highlight some materials needful in 'building a house.' He had seen it all, yet had seen nothing at all till he wrote his next book!

Wisdom, character, trust, goodness, co-ordination, vision, insight/foresight, resourcefulness, simplicity, chastity, kindness, generosity, simplicity, security, presentability, creativity, fairness, enterprise, strength, honour, patience, humility, perception, discretion, commitment, diligence, understanding, love and the fear of the LORD. These are some of the virtues essential in building, as Solomon puts it.

All praise and glory to God for how He is enabling Oluremi Ayida by His grace in performing her role of "building". Of a truth, it takes Him alone to build and establish as David, Solomon's father wrote earlier:

Except the Lord build the house they labour in vain that build it: except the LORD keep the city the watchman waketh but in vain.

Psalm 127:1

Paul also has this to say in one of his letters:

Brethren, I count not myself to have apprehended: but this one thing I do, forgetting those things which are behind, and reaching forth unto those things are before, I press toward the mark for the prize of the high calling of God in Christ Jesus.

Plilippians 3:13,14

There is a pressing. A working and walking on, that encapsulates every sphere of life. For Oluremi Ayida: "She is a caring and loving mother and grandmother. She lives for her children and grandchildren. She is a jewel of a wife. She truly cares," says her Prince of many, many years!

Speaking about her, Pastor Joel, a Minister and associate of the Friendship Bible Fellowship Ministries comments, "Like I said, she is very committed to God and work. She is also a down to earth woman, with special love for her children."

Oluremi Ayida, a veritable mother in Israel, has raised up not only her own children, but also several distant relatives and many others who are now well established in their own homes and businesses and who still fondly call her 'Mummy' to the praise and glory of God.

God has given grace over the years to live and pass on legacies from one generation to the other by the grace and mercy of God. Looking beyond the now and seeing into the future with the eyes of God. "Ma, can you describe briefly how it is, living a life for posterity?" I humbly asked Oluremi Ayida.

She prepared to give an answer as she adjusted her position more comfortably on her seat. She leaned backwards, paused and thought for a few seconds. Then she began.

"Well, when you are like a General Overseer or a leader, people should be able to remember something about you. Are you reliable? Are you disciplined? Do you have compassion? And when doing things, you don't do it as if you are doing something normal, an everyday thing, but with a purpose, a goal." She continued relaxed, but with firmness in her tone. "What I mean is this: to live for posterity, you must have a vision, if you don't have a vision, you will not arrive anywhere. So it's my goal that whatever I am doing I must leave something for people to see. I want people to see Christ in everything I do because it is only what you do for God's Glory that counts for posterity. Anything that I do, that does not glorify God is meaningless and counts for nothing. In building up people, ministry or raising children, all must be done through the help of God and wisdom that comes from Him alone. It is only God that can build for posterity, using me and my part is to yield my life to Him as a vessel for building. It is no longer I that is building for posterity but Christ in me (Galatians 2:20). By the grace of God I want to be remembered as a woman after God's heart; fully committed to serving Him. I want my life to challenge people working with me in God's Vineyard and in the secular world. I want to be remembered as a woman who pays close attention to what is good and one who strives to make the best choices. My challenge is choosing God and His ways and to be the one who encourages others to do so," she said as she ended answering the question.

Oluremi Ayida's life is expressed beyond her nucleus family. Her life reaches out in posterity to other people. Extended families, friends, associates, colleagues in career and ministry, even "strangers" are reached in one way or the other in fulfilling the divine purposes of her life.

She says, "When I came back from England, and settled in our own government accommodation, my mother-in-law came to stay with us, she did not come alone, but with some of her nieces and nephews, so that they could be brought up in a civilised environment and enjoy the benefit of a good education in Lagos. My husband is an only child, but his father had two other wives whose two children were very much younger than my husband. The two lovely girls were about five years of age when we took over their responsibilities. Biodun who is my mother-in-law's niece, was also with us at that time, she was less than a year when she came to stay with us. Her father had come to Lagos to see us and shortly after he returned, he died from an illness. Biodun's mother returned to her family leaving her children with my mother-in-law to care for.

She continued, "When my husband became Permanent Secretary, we had a bigger accommodation, I think we had about four boys' quarters. Sometimes we did not have less than ten people staying with us in the boys' quarters. They were all part of the extended families. For some, we were paying their school fees and for some, their parents would pay. So they all grew up with us."

Oluremi Ayida said it was a great responsibility on her then, because she had just started having her own children. "However, God was good to me, because He helped me to give my best to each of them. My two sisters-in-law graduated from University of Ibadan and Biodun from University of Ife (now Obafemi Awolowo University). They are all now well established in their various vocations and married with children. They all call me 'Mummy' and their children call me 'Grandma'. Raising these children has given me tremendous joy and a sense of fulfilment," she concluded.

Her husband, Mr Allison Ayida affirms this saying, "Mummy's role in dealing with extended family problems is exemplary. She does not distinguish between extended family on her side and mine. All our family is one. She handles the problems with prayers and service to humanity."

Mrs Alero Otobo, her first child, exhaustively and candidly spoke about their mother. Giving a brief description of her growing up, she stated that her childhood was full of memorable events. "I have fond memories of parents who are loving, kind and unbelievably generous. They gave us all we desired, and more. I remember in our early teenage years of going to visit Mummy at the Health centre – she was a very important Senior Health Sister. I remember with fondness, the snacks we ate, especially the boiled eggs. I also remember Fridays – they were special. Mummy always came home with comics and with the comics came chocolates and doughnuts." She continued, "Another major and memorable activity was travelling. We always went on wonderful family holidays. Within Nigeria we travelled to places of either historical or economic significance such as Kanji Dam (the first hydroelectric power plant), the Bacita sugar factory at Jebba, Delta steel plant in Warri, etc." Concluding, she stated that they had been to practically every country in Europe, to the United States and South America. She talked of the wonderful cruises they had had as a family crossing the Atlantic, the Mediterranean and for their father's seventieth birthday, the Caribbean. Mrs Otobo describes the family holidays as "incredible – a true blessing."

Recounting, she said as a teenager, she saw their mother as "a hardworking woman committed to her profession, a very generous person; there were so many uncles, aunties and cousins living with us when we were growing up – she must have had a generous spirit to welcome them all." Mrs Otobo added that their mum was strict and principled. "She taught us that a girl had to respect herself if she wanted to be respected by others," she says. I asked how she sees their mother now and her mother's influence in one or more areas of her life. Responding, she describes her as, "A precious woman of God whose love of God and desire to please Him never ceases to amaze me. A woman of wisdom who knows how to seek God's mind concerning issues and situations." She also referred to her mother as 'a woman of integrity.' She continues, "She taught us to do what is right. She taught us to respect our bodies, to love hard work and imbibe it as a core value." Speaking on challenging situations of her life and her mother's role in it, Mrs Otobo reveals that for every challenging situation, what stands out is how her mother supports her through prayer and the sharing of scriptures. "Just knowing that she is on her knees is always very comforting, and you know God answers her prayer!" she added with a sense of assurance. "Obviously you must have received dozens of gifts from Mummy, which are you most appreciative of?" I asked her.

"A wise and impactful book that she bought for each of us for our Christmas presents in 2003. The title of the book is *12 stupid mistakes people make with their money – and smart ways to avoid them* and in 2002 *A step by step guide to a secure financial future* by Dan Benson. The intention of the books is to make us better financial stewards," Mrs Otobo replied.

Certainly Oluremi Ayida is not a flawless angel. A true biography depicts a man's character and life: 'warts and all'. This truth cuts across the entire pages of this book.

Dr Mike Murdock states:

> "Greatness is not the absence of a flaw
> but the ability to survive the flaw."

Mrs Alero Otobo in responding to the candid question asked about their Mummy's weaknesses as they see it, said, she sometimes makes curt and sharp remarks that can be painful when someone says or does things she is not pleased with. Remarking Mrs Otobo says their mother needs to be more patient in her relationships especially with her household staff. We took a journey back to memory lane – when they were growing up. I asked Mrs Otobo if there were any events of note involving Mummy she could recall in these years of their young adulthood.

"Mummy collecting us from parties – she always waited patiently to pick us up and my parents' kind and positive treatment of our boyfriends. They were always nice to them – inviting them to even come on holidays with us. As a result boys always treated us with a great deal of respect and we never wanted to do anything that would displease or upset our parents."

Today, for Oluremi Ayida, her children rise up and call her blessed.

Mrs Alero Otobo concludingly describes the blessedness of their mother. "My mother has been an incredible blessing to all of us. A tower of strength, an intercessory powerhouse, a wise and understanding encourager, a beacon of light in the family, a creator of wealth, a builder of lives, she is a woman that has made history and continues to do so as she impacts lives."

For Oluremi Ayida she has come a long way by the grace of God and as a mother who with the support of her husband, have both raised up their children who are now established as families and have excelled in their fields of endeavour.

Oluremi Ayida also as a grandmother continues to stand as a positive and godly influence to her grandchildren as the word of God declares in Proverbs.

The silver-haired head is a crown of glory,
if it is found in the way of righteousness
16:31

Efena Otobo and Toluwalope Akerele are the second and fifth grandchildren respectively. They had so much to talk about concerning their grandmother, Oluremi Ayida.

Asked if there were any events of note in their lives or families involving Grandma that they always remember and the significance and effect of such. According to Efena she states, "About four years ago, Grandma gave me a beautiful *Bou-Bou* (Caftan). It was green and it was so beautiful. Choosing my secondary and my A level schools are areas of my life which are a great blessing today for which Grandma had an influence."

On her part, Toluwalope said, "In 1997 we moved house. My younger brother was born and we decided to move five months later as things were becoming cramped. Grandma flew in from Nigeria as soon as she could to come to bless our new house. She went through all four floors, rubbing oil on every door. At the time I thought nothing of it, but looking back, I realise how much of an effort Grandma must have made. Grandma has 'weak' knees, and climbing the stairs can only aggravate them. Yet, she went through each room in the house, all four floors and said a little prayer every time she stopped." She continued, "When I was younger, Grandma always brought me Topz Magazine. Grandma is a devout Christian and I always remember her because of her faith. So whenever I go to bed tired, I think of how Grandma would kneel to pray whilst I lie in bed. I would then say a little prayer before I slept. Although my family goes to church and prays, Grandma will go out of her way to make our faith stronger. For instance one day I needed a quotation from the King James Bible. The next day Grandma brought me the whole Bible to keep. By doing things like this, Grandma has taught me to share and be generous even when it is hard to do so."

Being teenagers that they are now I asked Efena and Tolu how they see their Grandma now, that is, their impression and perception of her.

For Toluwalope, "Grandma is someone very important in the extended family. She is the ideal role model for any young adult and the loving Grandmother a little child needs. But as a teenager, it is difficult to place words in how I view Grandma. She is an extraordinary person with a very energetic character for someone her age. I could not ask for a better Grandmother."

As for Efena, "I'm still a teenager," she said. She went on, "But even as a teenager, Grandma is a major influence in my life. With her guidance she has helped me make important decisions in my life. Right now Grandma keeps playing a major role in my life. She treats me like an adult even though I'm only seventeen!"

I asked the teenagers on what they consider as Grandma's weaknesses, knowing that as men, we must always acknowledge our frailties and inadequacies before God so that His strength is made perfect in our weakness and His righteousness through His Son may be revealed upon our lives.

For Efena, "Grandma can be quite stern and is easily angered at night."

Tolu puts it, "None that I can think of. Sometimes when Grandma scolds, she tends to scold quite harshly and does not realise when the person is upset. But when she does, she always hugs and tries to make amends."

Christ within us can accomplish what we can never hope to do in our own strength, and that continuous walking with Him will change the weakest of us into His image.

The blessedness of having such a loving Grandmother cannot be over-emphasised as the grandchildren described their Grandma.

In her golden words, Toluwalope says, "Her children rise up *because* she has blessed them. Grandma is very spiritual and has blessed me on numerous occasions. I am grateful and happy to have such a Grandmother."

Efena concludes with a heart of prayer for Grandma. "Grandma is a blessed woman. For years she has been a pillar of strength in my life. May she have many more years and may God grant her, her every wish, Amen."

> *Live in such a way as to pass something*
> *tangible to a new generation.*
> Lillian Trasher

5

HER PEACE

For God so loved the world that He gave His only begotten Son,
that whoever believes in Him should not perish but have
everlasting life.
John 3: 16

He is lodging with Simon, a tanner,
whose house is by the sea.
He will tell you what you must do.
Then Peter opened his mouth and said:
"In truth I perceive that God shows no partiality.
But in every nation whoever fears Him and works
righteousness is accepted by Him. The word which
God sent to the children of Israel, preaching peace
through Jesus Christ – He is Lord of all."
Acts 10: 6, 34 - 36

Peace in its literal sense has many connotations. It can be used to talk about a peaceful state or situation. A time of which there is no form of threat to the prevalent serenity and bliss of the environment. It could also be talked of as the state of being calm or quiet, having the peace of mind. The state of living in friendship with somebody can also be described as peace. Suffice it to say that people generally derive peace from the satisfaction they get or have per time from relationships, acquisitions, accomplishments or achievements of varying kinds without any form of threat to such. Any disturbance of this state by any threat whatsoever tends to bring with it such things as emotional instability, broken relationship, unhappiness, diseases, bankruptcy, violence, anarchy, war, loss, just to mention a few. It is a universal thing, it is the kind of peace that the world offers. It could be there today seemingly prevalent and predominant without any form of accusation or aggression, threatening or treachery, disturbance or distortion. However it could crumble like a pack of cards, completely reduced to non-existence because of the superficiality but true and lasting peace comes from God. It is only Him that gives such peace, one that is tenacious, not temporary.

Peace I leave with you, my peace I give unto you: not as the world gives, give I unto you ...

The Lord Jesus Christ

Speaking with Oluremi Ayida on what she believes to be the true state of peace, having and living in it. Starting, she takes us back to her life before she met the Lord. Taking a deep breath she began to narrate.

"Funny enough before conversion I had always thought of God. I had always offered my short prayer but still living in sin; telling little lies, cheating, doing all that, all those things were still on." Humorously, she added, "I did not know the difference between Jesus and God if there were any. That was me before conversion and I loved going out, going to a dance, as I loved dancing."

Mrs Ayida continued as I sat across her table all ears to what she said and intermittently jotting on my worksheet.

"I thought I could give myself peace of mind by doing certain things. If I don't tell lies I thought that would give me peace; or if I knew somebody and even if I didn't love the person, I pretended that I loved them just to be at peace. I thought I could earn peace by people loving me, and I would go that extra mile so that they could love me. But when I didn't go the extra mile the peace would go. I also felt I could earn peace by being sociable. I remember before I met Christ whenever I had any misunderstanding with my husband, I felt like going out to comfort myself, to give myself peace. I would go out shopping, I would blow off steam by just doing something, like eating what I shouldn't eat, just anything! That was my own impression of peace before I met Christ. I tend to work at peace, to make myself forget whatever problem there was and after getting what I thought could give peace, this peace sometime eluded me. It disappeared. I just could not find a solution to it. Then, I realise, there is more to getting peace than that."

As she continued speaking there was a knock at the door. It was Mr Mike a member of her staff. Standing by the door probably not wanting to take much time being conscious of the interview sessions, he gave her a reply in respect of a phone call she had asked to be made and left almost immediately closing the door gently behind him. I recalled that he had earlier been with her in the office together with two other staff members: Mr Godwin and 'Baba' (the Ministry's driver) as he is fondly called by all. They had been together when I arrived at her reception lounge, forty-five minutes earlier. We continued. Whilst thanking her for her time I began.

"This brings us to how you realised you needed Jesus or how you came to know Him by receiving the peace that comes from God alone." She responded by saying:

"My realisation of God was gradual. I think it had always been there. When we came back from England we were not attending church. It was only when we wanted to baptise the children: Alero and her younger sister that I went to Reverend Asekun, then at St. Judes Church. On one of my husband's official trips abroad, on his way back, he met an Australian couple in the boat, an expatriate architect who was coming to work in Lagos with the Ministry of Works. We became friends and started visiting one another. On one occasion, they asked where we worshipped and then invited us to Our Saviour's Church, Tafawa Balewa, Lagos also known as the Colonial Church. This was in 1961. I started attending church on their invitation." She continued,

"Immediately I left government service and retired as a Nurse in 1976 I became seriously ill that I had to be rushed to the Teaching Hospital. I thought I was going to die. There was an obstacle on the way there. It rained and everywhere was flooded. People could not move, our car was stuck that my husband had to carry me and waded through the water to get me to the hospital. The doctors couldn't remove my appendix because it was too bad, so they had to drain the abscess from it. I was unconscious but I got through it. Afterwards I thought: "Aha, there must be God in this, because I thought I was gone. Later on a colleague of mine visited me and said that she had dreamt over a month ago that she saw me. They were having my funeral but what she did was to get some friends, my colleagues and they went to a Catholic Church and they were praying to the Lord to ward away the death. When nothing happened after about a week, two weeks, three weeks they decided that everything was okay, until they now heard that I was at LUTH (Lagos University

Teaching Hospital). So the whole of the hospital where I worked as the Matron all came to visit me. But they had this peace because they had prayed and they took action when one of them had the dream. So when I look back now I see that the hand of God had always been on me. I've been waiting for something to just stir me up or to fill the vacuum. I've always been conscious of God, yet I was still living in sin. I was still living in the world, and I would say to myself, "I wish I knew how to read the Bible." I didn't know the Bible is something that I could pick up and start reading myself. I thought it was only the Pastors who should read the Bible. Satan just covered my eyes despite my age, intelligence and experience in life. I longed for somebody to teach me how to start. All I did then was to put it under my pillow and in the baby's cot, using the Bible as a 'charm' to protect us. My faith was in the book and not the word written in it so that was how I was doing my own thing. I was very worldly. I loved good things, spending, buying when I couldn't even afford it, thinking that it would make me feel good, look good and earn that peace that I craved for so much." The session was held up, as we had to give audience to Mrs Green, a leader and chairperson of Friendship Bible Coffees in the Ministry who came in at this time. Exchanging pleasantries with Mrs Ayida, the two had a brief conversation while I sat back. I guess we had needed that break to unwind a little. In no time we were back to business. Reminded of where we left off, she took off from there.

"... Not until I met the Lord. It was in 1982. My sister, Mrs Nanna, was invited to an FBC class by Mrs Bunmi Adeniji. Like Andrew now inviting his brother, (making her illustration from the Bible of Andrew's encounter with Jesus and telling of it to his brother Peter – John 1:40-42.) She came to tell me; "Sisi, (as she is fondly called by the elderly women) somebody has invited me to her house for a Bible study, would you like to come?" I said, "I have been hungry for something like this, let's go." For Oluremi, the invitation came as an answer to a quest she had had over some time. She continues. "So we went together. 'Who's that lady?' I asked my sister, wanting to confirm exactly whom it was. 'Mrs Bunmi Adeniji,' she replied." Mrs Ayida stated that they all belonged to the group that usually cleaned the church in their local assembly, a confirmation to what she had earlier asked her sister. On that particular day of church cleaning when Mrs Adeniji invited Mrs Nanna to the FBC Bible Study class, Oluremi was not present in the church. "At the first lesson of the FBC, it was on the study of Mark," she narrated. At the end of the study that day Oluremi said 'the guide' suggested that the class prepare for the next lesson by doing their homework in their study books. Whilst she was doing her homework she had an encounter. "The Bible speaks of 'a time to plant' (Ecclesiastes 3:2.) Friendship Bible Coffees (FBC) came as my time of planting. As I was reading and studying the book of Mark, I had a strong feeling inside of me convicting me of my sins. As I repented in tears I cried even more. I suddenly fell on my knees and surrendered my life to Christ, asking Him for forgiveness of my sins, I also asked Him to be my Lord and Saviour. At the end of my study that day, I felt inexpressible joy and peace flowing in my heart. God's Word is sharper than a double-edged sword." Oluremi Ayida recounted her conversion experience. She continued, "At the end of the study of the book of Mark we invited Pastor E. A. Adeboye, the General Overseer of 'The Redeemed Christian Church of God' to give us a talk. I have never heard anyone give such a clear exposition of the scripture in my life. At the end of his talk before he could finish making the altar call I was up on my feet. This was my first ever-public acknowledgement of Christ as my Lord and Saviour. It was the turning point in my life. I got back home and I could not stop crying. It was just like the feeling I had when I was doing my private study of the scripture. It was not the cry of sorrow but of joy; an inexpressible joy in my heart accompanied by a sense of inner peace. I had this great desire to hear people talking about or preaching the Gospel. I became very conscious of sin. Anytime I sinned I would lose my peace and become agitated and frightened. Gradually I started losing my appetite for sin."

Asking her, "What difference has Jesus made in your life – what's the difference between the past and the present, the old and the new?" With strength of conviction in her voice, Oluremi Ayida puts it this way, "Now I am dead to the world and it is no longer I in control of my life. I have surrendered my life to His control. The present is that now, my focus is not on myself or on what I can achieve or what I can do; but on what Christ can do through and in me and to tell people what I gain through Him, the benefits and how He has made the difference in my life."

"A walk of a lifetime," I prompted. She went on, "Before, I found that I could not help sinning. In a day I would have sinned about ten times, either by abusing somebody or by shouting or screaming or not forgiving. But gradually, it began to ease off and then I thought within myself, "Aha ha, listen Remi, it's one week now and you haven't sinned!" Before, sin was a part of me! But the minute I gave my life to Christ, He enabled me and gave me the power of His Holy Spirit to resist such temptations like covetousness. Before when I would see a person, I would want to be like them or want to have what they had. The Lord weaned me step by step, taking these bad habits away and He is still helping me. To get to this stage in my life has been a slow but gradual process and yet I have still not 'arrived'. Every day will be a new experience until I see my Lord face to face."

Now the works of the flesh are manifest, which are these; Adultery, witchcraft, hatred, variance, emulation's, wrath, strife, sedition's, heresies, envyings murders, drunkenness, revellings and such like: of the which I tell you before, as I have also told you in time past, that they which do such things shall not inherit the kingdom of God.
Galatians 5:19-21

Therefore if any person is (in-grafted) in Christ (the Messiah) he is a new creation (a new creature altogether); the old (previous moral and spiritual condition) has passed away. Behold the fresh and new has come!
2 Corinthians 5:17 (Amplified Bible)

Probably not to cut off the flow and tempo of the moment Oluremi did not pick up the phone that was ringing as she concluded, "I suppose the last one I will say is that I found impatience difficult to overcome. Satan always wants to have a stronghold over us but thank God, Jesus has set me free. I give all the glory to God. Though even now, I still sometimes struggle with it. In love I have seen God discipline me by allowing that which caused me to lose my cool to keep on happening to me until I cry to the Holy Spirit to help me. Now I hear the gentle whisper of the Holy Spirit warning me before 'I fly off the handle'. I thank God for the Holy Spirit who is very ready to help us in time of trouble."

It was a privilege accorded me by God to hear His handmaiden, Victoria Ayida. He began to draw on my heart how patient the Holy Spirit can be with us before He gets our attention.

Receiving the gift of Salvation is the greatest miracle that can happen to man. Jesus said in the thirty-sixth verse of the eight chapter of the book of Mark:

For what shall it profit a man, if he shall gain
the whole world and lose his own soul?

God's general, Reverend Kenneth Hagin says: "No man in his right mind would plunge himself out into eternity without God." God has called every man into the ministry of reconciliation because God in Christ reconciled and restored the world to favour with Himself, not counting up and holding against men their sins but cancelling them and committing to everyone the message of being reconciled to Him (II Corinthians 5:19). When one has made peace with God through Christ he receives the peace of God, with men and with oneself.

Unmerited favour, undeserved grace, JESUS alone has lifted me,
from the dungeon to marvellous light.
Mike Chiadika

Father: Mr Law Cheke

Mother:
Alhaja Ajiwun Dosunmu

With Mrs Tinu Madarikan,
a childhood friend

Remi at eighteen years old

Family A

As student nurse, 1951 with
colleague Miss Yinka Cole

Bride, 1957

Marriage Day
September 1957

Family B

Family in 1974

Family C

*Right: With sister
Mrs Toritseju Esther Nanna (left)*

*Below: Family Planning Visit,
Pakistan, 1968*

*Brownie
pack, 1967*

Family/Career D

*At retirement
send-off
reception in 1976*

*Presentation
of gift at
retirement
send-off by
Nursing sister
Mrs Sowande
in 1976*

*With Mrs Akinsete,
as Fellow of West African
College of Nursing
(FWACN)*

Mr Allison Ayida,
husband, 2005

30th Wedding Anniversary
Marriage Blessing at All Souls'
Church, Langham Place,
London, 1987

Evening Celebration
of 30th Wedding Anniversary
in Venice

Family F

Above left: Oluremi as a proud Grandmother

Above: Allison and Oluremi, Christmas 2006

Left: from bottom left: Mrs. Alero Otobo, Mr. Abidemi Ayida. 2nd row: from left: Daddy, Mummy and Mr Maje Ayida, top from left: Mr Omatseyin Ayida and Dr (Mrs) Gbubemi Ayida-Akerele at Christmas, 2006

Grandpa and Grandma with the grandchildren at Christmas, 2006

Family G

Mr & Mrs Ayida in traditional Itsekiri attire at an occasion in Warri, 2006

Testimony of Daughter's car accident

Family H

6

HER PASSION

And certain women who had being healed
of their evil spirits and infirmities-
Mary called Magdalene, out of whom
had gone seven demons, and
Joana wife of Chuza, Herod's steward,
and Susanna, and many others who provided
for Him from their substance.
Luke 8: 2-3

And being in Bethany at the house
of Simon the leper,
as He sat at the table, a woman came
having an alabaster flask of very
costly oil of spikenard. And she broke
the flask and poured it on His head.
"She has done what she could. She has come
beforehand to anoint My body for burial."
Mark 14: 3, 8

Passion is a thing, act or course for which somebody has great enthusiasm for. It is rightly said to be a strong feeling and a pointer to discovering purpose. Speaking with Oluremi Ayida on what she believes to be her passion she responded.

"My passion is that I just want to be with Him all the time. I found that I was no more interested in the worldly way of life; going to parties, buying *aso ebi*, (uniformed wears for occasions), my old friends started seeing me as a religious fanatic;" she spoke emphatically as she continued.

"My joy is full when I am in His presence, that is, communicating with my heavenly Father; spending quality time in His presence. I have peace when I am fellowshipping with other believers, praising and worshipping God. My passion is also in reading and studying the word of God and listening to renowned men of God preaching and teaching the Word of God. I desire so much to emulate them in serving God," says Oluremi. Narrating the expressions of her enthusiasm and zeal with which she began to serve God after her conversion, Oluremi Ayida recounted those times. "As a new convert, my desire to know God was so intense that I used to attend every Christian crusade and convention I heard about both in Nigeria and abroad. This hunger took me everywhere where they were calling God. I wanted to go here and there, to the extent that I sometimes felt guilty that every day of the week was occupied. For three years running I attended Rev. Kenneth Hagin camp meetings in Oklahoma, USA. I travelled to Orlando also in the USA to worship at Pastor Benny Hinn's church. I travelled to England to be at Billy Graham and Oral Robert's Crusades. I attended the Holy Ghost service at the Redemption camp, Lagos listening to Pastor Adeboye. With other friends I organised pilgrimages to Lourdes in France, a Catholic Retreat centre. For all the places I have been to, I have always had friends to join me." With keen interest and surprise I exclaimed, "You've attended all those Christian meetings abroad!" Interestingly and excitingly she continued, "I distinctly remember one of the programmes I attended in London in the company of God's servant, Pastor Adeboye." Speaking in a lighter tone, with visible expression of joy and inner fulfilment, she went on, "Pastor Adeboye is one of my favourite Pastors and my father in the Lord. I have learnt a lot from him especially lessons in humility and clarity in preaching. I remember when he was in London during one of my visits, I went to visit him where he was staying with a member of his congregation. I asked 'Daddy' if he would like to come with me to Billy Graham's crusade, (held at Earls Court arena), as I had an extra invitation to share. I was not expecting him to accept my invitation but to my delight Daddy agreed. I was on top of the world to be attending a crusade with this General of God. I felt highly honoured and I could not stop thanking God for this opportunity accorded me to learn a great lesson in humility."

Oluremi's passion for God could be said now to be the foundation of which all other aspects stand. It is the passion that laid the basis on which the Friendship Bible Coffees (FBC) and Every Day with Jesus (EDWJ) stands. As she puts it, "The hunger is what has drawn me so much to FBC that I have taken it as if it is 'a do or die'. I must breathe it, nurture it. I must do whatever I can do despite all the persecutions and challenges."

However, I drew back her attention to the zeal she had as a new believer in the early days which made her attend every possible programme as long as it had to do with God. I remarked that it was not every gathering that calls 'God' that is of God! How then was she able to decipher where the Spirit of God wanted her to go or not to go?

She responded, "As I grew and moved closer to the Lord, the Spirit of God ministered to me that He wanted me not to concentrate on attending meetings and crusades, but to concentrate on reading His Word and getting others to do so as well. Probably that was why He led me to be born again through His Word as I was studying the Bible and doing my homework. I want people to experience Him as they read His Word."

So from the light of God's revelation to her heart, she started cutting down attending meetings and crusades. "So instead of inviting friends with me to go to crusades, I now invite them to Bible studies (FBC)," she concludes restfully.

The heart of generosity well reported by many concerning Oluremi Ayida was the next area of her passion we spoke on.

I commented that the heart of liberality was given by God to complement the passion she has for Him and the work. Making reference to the women in the eighth chapter of Luke the second and third verses the Bible says after their various life changing encounters with the Lord Jesus they ministered unto Him of their substance. Responding modestly she puts it.

"Mine is that I love giving to the Lord, anything that is of God, anything that is to the Kingdom of God I love giving towards it. Even if I don't have, the little I do have I can give ninety percent of it to Him leaving the rest for me. That is my joy, remembering that no one can out-give God."

She recalled how she was given a plot of land by her Aunt in Warri on which she built a duplex. While she gave a wing of it to the family, the other was let out. After sometime there was a backlog on rent payment and the tenant refused to vacate the property. She said she took the case to God in prayer, vowing that if the man would leave she would give the apartment to the parish of the Redeemed Church of God. She had learnt that the church was presently worshipping in someone's garage somewhere in Warri. To her surprise the man who refused to go just came and paid up arrears owed and left. When she learnt of it on her return from an overseas trip and that the apartment was vacant, the place was quickly given to the church as a starting point in Warri from which other parishes have also emerged.

"So I like to give to the Almighty, to the cause of God. The glory goes to God, because it is He who works in me to will and to do His will. He puts the desire in me." She continued speaking as she testifies of God's faithfulness in meeting her at the point of her need.

"I derive joy in giving to the Lord because He always multiplies the gift beyond my expectation. Our God is a great God," she revealed narrating her personal experience, "And I have never lacked. Even when I give as much as ninety percent of what I have, God always meets my needs, in one way or the other the Lord always replenishes. So I always like to do that. And when He calls you to give He knows there is a need coming and when you agree to do His will, He rewards you by filling your cup to overflowing as He says in Luke *6:38 "Give and it shall be given unto you; good measure, pressed down, shaken together and running over, shall men give into your bosom for with the same measure you mete withal it shall be measured to you again."* He meets you and when you agree and you give, He will fulfil that need before you. He is not a debtor to anybody. There is no time I have given that He has not overwhelmed me. So there is nothing to give because as you give, straightaway He is replenishing. If not materially or financially, you'll see it in other aspects of your life."

God's servant Dr David Oyedepo, says,

"I'm not giving to support God
He is too Big to need my support
I'm giving to support my destiny on earth ..."

On retirement from the civil service Oluremi Ayida recalled that her pension was about five hundred naira but God has always been providing for her. Even that which she gives has been the provisions of God as she says, "He makes someone give it to me. I think He opens a pipeline, just to pass the provision through me and this is what I want people to realise. That when we do have He is making us a channel, we are just stewards to be accountable to Him and when we don't use it to His glory, then we're in trouble."

On how she gives her talent and time just like she gives her treasure to that which she believes in life and in ministry. She began. "Now I can sit back and see that the Hand of God has been in my life. Before I became a Christian, anywhere I am, even as a little girl, I have always taken a leadership role. In one thing or the other, people would just pick me out to lead, and because God has given me that grace I always succeed. So I think this is a talent from God. Added to that is discipline. I trained as a Nurse. A Public Health Nurse has to be disciplined and sympathetic to be able to care for patients. So, that training I had for several years, helped me to have this discipline; to be punctual, to be on duty; to take my work seriously and enjoy what I do in commitment." "All these are now being harnessed for God's work at this time of your life," I remarked harmoniously. On her time, Oluremi Ayida comments:

"When I retired, I started doing some home decorations and furnishing but I wasn't satisfied and then FBC came up. Immediately I gave up everything, although I was making good money but I was no more interested in it. I was more interested in the one I didn't make a penny from. I think it is God that has really captured me," she said.

There was a gentle laugh from me at the choice of her word describing her call into divine assignment, even though her tone signified depth from her soul. Speaking further, she said, "Every minute I have now, I just want to give it to the Lord. If I have three things to do, and only one is for God, I will do that one first. If the time that I have does not cover all the things I need to do, I will use that time to do the one for the Lord. It has been my motto that 'God first'. He is my heavenly priority. Anything that is pertaining to God, the ministry, to my spiritual life, that is my number one choice," she said.

For Oluremi Ayida, God has given her much passion for Him, His work and for people. Sowing seeds of love, peace, patience, mercy, time and money by perception and healthy relationships has a profound place in her heart, which she sees as a privilege and she's grateful to God for this.

But the fruit of the Spirit is love, joy, peace, long-suffering, gentleness, goodness, faith, meekness, temperance: against such there is no law.
Galatians 5:22-23.

One of Dr Mike Murdock's wisdom nuggets says:
"An uncommon seed creates an uncommon harvest
You are a walking collection of seeds.
Something you've been given to get what you've been promised."

At the helm of affairs of a successful Christian organisation her upward relationship with God and downward relationships with men are vital to achieving success. However, it is the success of the upward relationship that is released to the downward one. I asked Oluremi Ayida, "How has God been helping you build healthy relationships with people, the place of perception, discernment and judgement with people?"

"When I meet anyone, my first thought and desire is to influence the person for Christ, to tell them about Christ and His love. I feel that a life without Christ is a wasted life and no one should waste God's given life in this world. Everybody needs Christ and all people should be aware of this. A lot of people do not know that salvation is free. They need to be told. Everyone must hear the 'Good News'. It is amazing that most churchgoers are not saved. They know about Christ, but they don't have Him in their lives or allow Him to rule their lives." Oluremi tenaciously went on speaking, "I was a churchgoer for over twenty years, but only came to the knowledge of His saving grace after well over forty years of age. I was aware of His existence at an earlier age in life but it had made no impact on me. It was an experience that quickly disappeared. Because of my own experience I stopped assuming that every churchgoer is a Christian. I have made it my business to influence anyone I meet for the first time for Christ. I would start off a conversation that leads to me testifying of the Love of Christ and His saving Power. If my new friend has a need I would say a quick quiet prayer for God to use me to meet their need, by the end of our encounter a seed of salvation would have been sown even if I didn't lead my new friend to Christ. Wherever possible I try to follow up by inviting them to an FBC class or by sending them a copy of *Every Day With Jesus* or *Inspiring Women Every Day*. I like encouraging people to be fervent in their relationship with the Lord not lukewarm, for a lukewarm Christian backslides easily. I always ask God to use me to meet the needs of people in order to draw them closer to Christ. Whenever a sister in Christ is celebrating an occasion I make it my duty to be there if I am available. Even when I am tired, God always gives me the strength to attend the occasion and I do my part of making the effort to go. The Lord always blesses me by making the response of the sister to my effort so overwhelming, that they start giving their own time to serving the Lord in the ministry. It is the Lord's work in the person's heart. This is God's doing and it is marvellous!" she said. Giving another instance of this she went on, "If someone comes to me saying they need help, maybe the person has not been paid their salary or is in debt, I always try to help with whatever I can afford. I do not give personal loans. If you need a thousand naira I can perhaps give you two hundred naira as led by the Holy Spirit, recognising that love must be shown in action. This is what drives me, the love of Christ because you can't see Christ. You can't see His hands but we are His hands, we are His feet. In giving I have learnt to pray to God to direct my giving. Whatever I give is usually appreciated even when it is small," she concluded.

I recall a statement made by God's Servant Dr Tunde Bakare saying:

"Relationship is the currency of the spirit ..."

Having adequate perception of people, of who they are and seeing them with the eyes of God goes a long way; and God uses this to reach out to them and doing things even beyond man's comprehension. This however sometimes may not be without its own challenges.

Commenting on this Oluremi Ayida puts it:

"It is only God who is at work in me. I have no power of my own. It's only God that does it because if not for God I would have given up."

"Definitely! Because you are human!" I added. "I'm human!" she responded agreeing with the truth of man's inadequacies. She continued:

"Consistency, despite the challenges."

Almost immediately I remembered something I had read a few days back in the Inspiring Women Everyday devotional. Bringing it out from my bag I opened to the page and read out:

"And a heart woven into the True Vine will produce exactly what it's meant to - excellent grapes!

Veering off to focus on how your Christian life is looking to others is a killer ..."

"It's a killer!" she exclaimed.

I continued reading from the prayer portion:

"Lord, help me to stop fussing about what other people think. Help me get my heart right instead."

"That has been my motto, "Lord, help me to stop fussing about what other people think," she responded. "And that is what I tell my co-labourers in God's vineyard. Let us focus our eyes on Christ and do what He has committed into our hands to do. Everyone should do what they can with a sincere heart. Ignore irrelevant issues, focus on things that build, not one that pulls down. God gives patience to tolerate sarcasm, gossips, etc. until differences are resolved and unity established and everyone is working towards the goal. When we are united it pleases God and delights His heart. So every servant in God's vineyard must strive for unity. It is through unity of purpose that we achieve the goal of our vision." I quietly sat listening to the depth of godly understanding that flowed from Oluremi. "Every servant of God is bound to meet discouragement now and again, but we should never give in to discouragement; accept criticism graciously knowing that if God is with you, who can be against you? No one! What matters is, what Christ thinks about you! Always take time to examine your service to the Lord. Are you still glorifying God in your service to Him? All we do must be to His glory, not to ourselves or to man. When we are working for His Glory, He orders and directs our actions and prospers whatever we do, whether great or small. God grants His children favour and acceptance, knowing that He is the One that matters and that in pleasing Him, you'll find peace with man."

" The life God has given you is not as if you've even chosen it," I remarked. "No!" she punctuated.

I went on, "God who is in us, uses us, to do what He wants, through us. It's a life of obligation, discipline and shared sufferings. He prepares you for that which He has prepared for you to do."

Picking up the conversation Oluremi adds with strong emphasis in her voice, "One thing I have discovered is that when God calls you, there is no way of escape. Despite all opposition He will grant you that grace to bear it and surmount all obstacles in your way. The task He gives you becomes easy when you are willing to obey Him. He meets all your needs and opens doors of favour for the success of the tasks He has committed into your hands. He strengthens His character in you not to react to the abuse and unfavourable remarks. He just removes the pain of gossip and fills our hearts with peace. It is a mystery, our hearts have to be right."

One other aspect of Oluremi's life of passion is her enthusiasm of having people around her. Joyfully she says, "I like having people around me. I like my family around me. I passionately promote the well-being of my husband, my family and all other people that God has placed in my life. Any opportunity to have a party I use it to glorify God in worship and praying together, giving testimonies of God's goodness in our lives. I seize the event to proclaim Christ such as turning a birthday party into an outreach, turning FBC holidays to pilgrimages to the Holy Land, turning the Mediterranean cruise to a Christian cruise and at Christmas times we have an open house. It gives me so much joy to hear our grandchildren taking turns to pray. O how I glorify God to hear our four-year old grandson praying for his teachers, friends, parents, and other people. My passion is to interact with them, share together and laugh together."

Love that goes upward is worship.
Love that goes outward is affection.
Love that stoops is grace.
Donald Barnhouse

7

HER PURPOSE

… For this cause I was born,
and for this cause I have come into the world,
that I should bear witness to the truth…
John 18:37

For David, after he has served
his own generation
by the will of God, fell asleep, was buried
with his fathers, and saw corruption.
Acts 13:36

I started off describing purpose as an inner force without which lasting success and accomplishment would be impossible. Purpose gives meaning to one's life. "You can't put a round peg in a square hole!" so goes the popular saying. God has a purpose for every man He has created. Not knowing the reason for one's creation will mean an abuse of one's time, talent, treasure and training. On a gradual note, God makes our purposes known to us as we seek Him and He is committed to it. Purpose is the thing, which won't leave one alone. It is that constructive imagination that keeps driving one on, the idea that keeps coming back over the years.

Many plans are in a man's mind, but it is the
Lord's purpose for him that will stand.
Proverbs 19:21 (Amp.)

It was one of the sessions we had on her return from the long trip to the USA for the leadership summit at the StoneCroft Ministries in Kansas City with some other members of the ministry.

Talking about her understanding, inspiration, motivation and discovery of her purpose Oluremi Ayida states, "My purpose is to see believers grow in the knowledge and love of God through reading and studying the word of God as it is the only way to grow in faith.

This is what God has called me to do. To please God and know His will for your life is through His Word! As a new Christian I was on fire for the Lord, I wanted every friend of mine to attend fellowship with me or crusades or Holy Ghost services but God's Spirit witnessed to my spirit that I should focus my zeal on inviting people to Bible study. Even when it was being suggested that we form a church I said "No". This is why I concentrate more on FBC and the distribution of reading aids – *Every Day With Jesus* (EDWJ) and other aids for those who do not attend Bible study. They benefit from using the devotionals. The ministry also distributes tracts by the "StoneCroft Life Publications" to create an awareness of salvation through Christ. EDWJ and our other Bible reading aids helps the ministry to reach out to people who find it difficult to join FBC study groups. I remember once travelling to Jos to encourage some group of ladies to start an FBC Bible study group. It started well but lasted for less than a year. I then got them interested in EDWJ, now we have more than one distributor in Jos and the readership is growing. Where we cannot get to, EDWJ is getting there!"

She spoke convincingly of what she believes to be her purpose. Pausing, she asked me, "Are you reading the current edition on EDWJ?" (Referring to the July / August 2004 of EDWJ on *Spiritual Sure Footedness*) almost immediately she carried on, "It ministered so much to me. People especially the Bankers who were going through difficulties of change testified of how this edition ministered to them in diverse ways to calm their hearts. This was the period the Federal Government passed the law that the asset base for commercial banks should now be 25 billion naira in less than two years from that date. Some bank asset bases were not even up to five billion naira. I remember that my husband and I were having our devotion with EDWJ when we received the news. The passage of the scripture we were studying was Isaiah 41:10-14 and God spoke to us through verse 13 "Fear not, I myself will help you..." (paraphrased). We received the promise with joy and held on to the verse and God has truly helped us. Those banks that turned to God for guidance made it. The teaching of that edition was to commit our fears concerning the change to God in prayer for His guidance and to direct our paths to success. My heart leaps for joy when I hear people testifying to the change of their attitude to God. The comfort that He has given them through *Every Day With Jesus*. The counsels received in difficult times directing them in making a choice and calming the storms of life. I have many testimonies of people attesting to this. A lady who lost her husband in the Port – Harcourt to Lagos plane crash a few years ago testified that God used EDWJ to comfort her. She is now a missionary winning souls for the Lord. The Bible reading notes for that period were on the loss of loved ones. EDWJ ministers not only to lay Christians but also to seasoned Ministers who use it as one of their Bible reading aids. With the FBC study groups and distribution of EDWJ, God is glorified and He must feel good. I just say "Father, Glory be to Your Name. To You be all the glory and praise, honour and adoration." I rested comfortably on the chair as I sat back listening to Oluremi Ayida as she spoke intermittently making gestures to create a lasting memory. Every word came with strength. I felt the air of reverence and joy of fulfilment. "It is not me it is God's will as He is doing something and my prayer is that God Almighty will continue to promote FBC and the devotionals. That this move of God would get to every home in Nigeria; Christians, Muslims, pagans and that they will meet Christ through it, as I met Christ through reading the Bible. I have heard of Muslims reading EDWJ. We have had Muslims becoming members of FBC and still are. FBC is a non-denominational Bible study group. Our focus is JESUS not on denomination. As we grow together in the studies we become united in Him. We are sisters and brothers in Christ. FBC is a life changing Bible study. It has so much impact on members' lives that Christ shines through you and you start behaving like Christ at home and in your community. People note the changes in you and most of the husbands have testified to this and surrendered their lives to Christ. Before I joined FBC I was attending church alone, my husband only went to church when he was invited to weddings, or any other Christian ceremony. However through my consistency, faith and change in my behaviour and through answer to prayers, God changed his life and we now worship God together at home and at church. Praise the Lord! The glory goes to God. To get my husband to give his life to Christ took over twelve years of my crying day and night to God in prayers. God first 'off-loaded' me of my self-centredness, removed all my bad habits and my self-dependence. It was when I was totally broken that the Almighty God took over and brought my husband to his knees as he surrendered his life to Christ. Our God is a great God and His mercy endures forever, but for His mercy my husband would have died and gone to hell!" She said with deep satisfaction and joy.

God is described as the God of purpose. The purpose of a thing is its glory. The bird is created to fly; the fish to swim, that's the place of fulfilment.

"God has put you in this ministry because He knows what He will do through you concerning the reading of His Word spreading to this nation and beyond. So even before you went into the Christian Organisation of the Friendship Bible Coffees; sometime in the past, through your Nursing Career, you must have perceived your purpose? It had always been there, though waiting for the timing of God to be understood and seen."

She reflects, then maintains that she derives joy when she is helping people. If there were anything she could do either by giving advice or counselling people or resolving issues between two parties that might even be older than herself she finds herself readily doing it.

"I love being helpful and God always puts me in a situation that I can exercise that gift," she said softly.

She stated that in respect of the EDWJ publication, the author, Reverend Selwyn Hughes was looking for a way of reaching more people. Immediately he was approached he readily affirmed that we (the ministry) were the group he was looking for, a Christian group that was not a church.

Her desire she says is always to be of help to anyone with a need. She recalled an incidence in her nursing days. "I've sat with a mother who thought her child was dead and had run away. By the grace of God the child was revived and was now all right. However the mother had unconsciously taken the medical card with her when she left. So I had to sit with the child all day till the evening when the father came to claim the body but it was joy all over. God opens my eyes to see a need and draws my heart to desire to meet the need. I love being a blessing to people because it is already there by God," she concludes.

Suffice to say that every call of God is preceded by a divine purpose; a fulfilment of an assignment which will require divine intervention and input.

Who has saved us and called us with a holy calling, not according to our works, but according to His own purposes and grace which was given to us in Christ Jesus before time began.
2 Timothy 1:9

I am the vine, you are the branches. He who abides in Me and I in him bears much fruit; for without Me you can do nothing.

John 15:5

At this we appreciated the realisation of her purpose made possible by God acknowledging that as men we easily stray and in which we so often stumble and divert but for the grace of God that is revealed. It is expected that we fulfil God's plan and purpose for our individual life. We are not to run someone else's race or finish someone else's course for God has set a different course before each of us. We are to be what He wants us to be.

Oops! We had come to the end of the day's business, it had been a rainy day. As we rounded up preparing to take my leave Mrs Akande, the Account Staff, came in for her usual round-up on the day's returns. Exchanging greetings we all called it a day.

The end result of purpose is glory.
Dr Tunde Bakare

8

HER POWER

God has spoken once,
Twice have I heard this:
That power belongs to God.
Psalm 62:11

But you shall receive power when the Holy Spirit
has come upon you; and you shall be witnesses
to Me in Jerusalem, and in all Judea
and Samaria, and
to the end of the earth.
Acts 1:8

It was a bright Tuesday in September. The earlier cloud patches in the sky had disappeared. I got to the headquarters in the mid-afternoon. Though a little behind schedule but right on time for the interview session. She was already in the office. I waited in the secretary's office for another half-hour giving her enough time to get through with her lunch. Shortly after she told Ms Ifeoma, the administrative secretary, to ask me in. I went straight to her office, knocking at the door and opening almost immediately I went in, closing the door gently behind me. Greeting her in the usual manner, she responded welcoming me in. I took my seat on one of the two chairs across her table bringing out a few sheets of white paper from my work bag, my pen and of course my little recorder, set for work we commenced.

I remarked. Many people are encouraged and challenged at the way they see you at your present age; God has equally given you this kind of voluminous work that you do on a daily basis both at the home front and in the ministry. What is the source of power by which you live this strong and remarkable life?

Responding in a soft tone Oluremi Ayida replied:

"The first thing, the power is from God not from me. The joy of serving the Lord gives me strength. When I know that I am doing something for the Lord I just put all that is in me into it and when I am tired I lay down to rest and by the following day it's as if I didn't do anything. So I see that the source of my strength is not me. It's not because I'm eating well or because I'm exercising. Yes I eat well!" she added promptly as if not to undermine the essence of good feeding.

"I try to watch what I eat and I try to do exercises and when I was able I used to swim, but that is not the strength that gets me going. God is the one that has given me that ability. God is the primary source of that power. It is by His grace that I enjoy good health at my age. I don't pant going up and down, it's from God."

"Basically the power comes from within from the strength of the Spirit of God within you," I added, as we both made reference to God's word.

"God hath spoken once; twice have I heard this; that power belongeth to God; But ye shall receive power after that the Holy Ghost is come upon you ..."

At this, I went on to ask her on how she envisions or see the Person of the Holy Spirit that gives her the power. How she cultivates His Presence as He supplies the power she needs spiritually, physically, emotionally and mentally to do those exploits. Speaking she puts it this way:

"What I have discovered is that the Holy Spirit is there to be our strengthener and every time before I perform any task I call on the Holy Spirit to help me and give me the strength ..."

The phone rang. She picked it and had to speak with a prospective distributor of the devotional books and concluded arrangements on how the person would get the supplies.

We continued the conversation, "So I always appeal to the Holy Spirit to help me, to give me strength. I have a testimony to give about the Holy Spirit. I remember once, years ago. Two co-ordinators from two different groups had a misunderstanding. They were going to have a joint outreach and if they didn't co-operate the outreach would be a flop. This was on a Thursday; I was travelling the following day to Warri early in the morning. I was told to come over to the groups or else they would not co-operate. I went straight on my knees and I asked the Holy Spirit to take control over everything, that He should minister to them and bring peace to the situation. After my prayer I had peace and I went on my journey to Warri. By the time I got back a day before the joint outreach the two co-ordinators had settled their differences amicably without the help of anyone. I learnt later that the Holy Spirit convicted both of them. They arranged to meet and settled their differences. The outreach was a great success, to God be the glory who does everything so beautifully more than any man can ever do. That is the power of the Holy Spirit. From this experience, I now always ask the Holy Spirit to help me to accomplish my task and He never fails. Whenever we attend conferences either in the UK or the USA I am always asked to speak for our group from Nigeria. Even when I nominate someone to do it, they always still want me to share with them. At this point I go on my knees and ask the Holy Spirit to speak through me. It is amazing when He takes over. The message flows, my inadequacy disappears because it would not be me talking but the One above. At times I cannot even remember what I have said to the audience which could be more than 1,500 Christians from different countries of the world. The Holy Spirit has never let me down. What He does for me now is to inform me before the gathering that I would be called to speak or to say a prayer, so that I can prepare myself but all the same He is still the One that does it through me. Very recently I was getting ready to attend one of the high society birthday receptions; the Holy Spirit dropped in my heart that I would be called upon to pray. When it was time, the Master of Ceremony went to an important, respected gentleman to ask him to pray. I thought I did not hear from the Holy Spirit thinking that I had heard my own thoughts, but a few seconds later the M.C. also came to me and asked if I could pray because the gentleman had told him that he would rather I prayed. What a friend I have in the Holy Spirit! I am indeed very grateful for the numerous ways Jesus Christ has been leading me through His Holy Spirit. I am indeed very humbled before Christ for changing my inadequacy to His adequacy; glory be to His Name."

It is said that the Holy Spirit enlightens, He envisions and also empowers. Asked to further let us in into events or happenings on how He does this in her life by giving her understanding or goals and the ability to implement such and achieving the desired result.

She began, "On a daily basis, He just drops something in my heart," she paused for a moment as if trying to recall an appropriate instance. "He enlightens me. Do you know He inspired me as to the plan of this building? (Referring to the headquarters). I prayed to God to show me what He required in the building. When I woke up in the morning ideas came to my mind concerning the building. The first thoughts were on different departments of the ministry and their requirements. From there, comes the thought of room space required for each, and then the supporting amenities for each department. The number of rooms required determined the number of floors the building would have. I jotted my ideas down as the Holy Spirit dropped them into my heart. Whatever I overlooked the Holy Spirit would drop into a member's heart who would then come to tell me."

For as many as are led by the Spirit of God,
they are the sons of God.
Romans 8:14

She went on to say how the Holy Spirit grants her illumination, direction and guidance as she seeks to walk in God's purpose for her life. Oluremi Ayida recounted the time she had to go to the StoneCroft Ministries in America in 1999 to explain herself in relation to the activities of the Friendship Bible Coffees in Nigeria. The leadership had sent a letter to Nigeria to stop all FBC activities there because they had been informed that there had been a digression from the StoneCroft policies. "The FBC committee in Nigeria suggested that I should go to StoneCroft to explain our side of the story. At first I refused to go, I wanted to just put my reply in writing but the Holy Ghost prompted me to go with one or two members. Before we left for Kansas City we fasted and prayed and I wrote down everything concerning the FBC activities, projects and developments so far. I travelled with Mrs Nanna and Mrs Green. The night before our meeting with them we submitted our report. The next day the three of us that went there and three of the leadership team there met together. Mrs Green spoke, Mrs Naana spoke and I spoke. We all then started to pray one after the other. The place was charged with the Presence of God and some of the panel started to cry. At the end of the prayer, the Chief Executive of StoneCroft Ministry, Joyce Courtney, said, "Remi, we are satisfied with what you are doing in Nigeria…" Without further debate and explanation they gave us their

60

approval and blessing to continue with the FBC ministry in Nigeria and anything that would enhance its progress. We discovered that some of our activities have now been adapted as part of Stonecroft's. We give the glory to God. During this time of trial the Lord was with us, with the Holy Spirit guiding us each step of the way. Instead of dismissing the FBC ministry in Nigeria the Lord used it to promote us. More consulting co-ordinators were appointed in Nigeria." She promptly added:

"So this last summit we attended, the first day was allotted to us to speak. Mrs Omatsone, Mrs Green and myself gave our talk. The presentation was well received. On occasions when I am called to speak without prior notice I just whisper to the Holy Spirit for His help to give me His inspiration and the wisdom and usually at the end of my presentation I would receive a standing ovation. That is the work of the Holy Spirit," she spoke interestingly.

Oluremi ascribes the relationships the ministry has had so far in enhancing and expanding the work to the Holy Spirit. Speaking of one such incidence she said she felt the need for the leadership and membership of the ministry to be more equipped in the word of God to enhance personal growth and service in the Lord's work. After deliberation she personally approached the General Overseer of the Redeemed Christian Church of God. She requested for a satellite Bible College to be situated at the Ministry's headquarters. Responding he explained to her that there was only one for the entire church which was on the Camp ground for everyone to attend. However after he had met with the governing board of the church they gave the permission to start a satellite Bible College at the FBC headquarters which took off in October 1990. To date it remains the only independent college outside of the Redeemed Christian Church organisation; the church Pastors conduct the lectures, activities and awards of certificates. The first graduation from the college was on the 4th of August 1993 where Oluremi Ayida also finished as a graduate. Since then the Redeemed Christian Church has also opened several other satellite Bible Colleges.

The Handmaiden of God, Oluremi Ayida for who she is and will ever be in Christ owes all to the Spirit of God. Over the years she has not only come to know the Person of the Holy Spirit but has treasured a priceless and revered relationship with Him who is the strength of her being.

She further revealed of her relationship with Him, "When I'm addressing the Holy Spirit I address Him as 'my best friend', He is always at my side. When I call Him my 'best friend' He is always there to show me, tell me, and direct me." She made reference to an incidence that happened in her local assembly and the need to settle that matter.

"I needed to see the Chairman of the Parish council. He lived in Mushin. Nobody could describe the place to me. They couldn't get the address but said the house was on top of Lennards Shoe Shop in Mushin! I prayed and the Holy Spirit said to me, "The first person you stop to ask will direct you". So I told my driver we're going to look for Lennards Shoe shop at Mushin. Mushin is a big place. I felt I should go to the Local Government office there, where they would direct me to the place. As we entered a road I saw a man standing wearing *Danshiki* (a type of local attire) by the roadside. I said to my driver, 'Stop! stop!' I said to the man: "My brother 'Jo' (means, 'please', in the Yoruba language) I'm looking for Lennards Shoe Shop." The man gave a good description of the place. The first person I talked to! Probably he was an angel," she added humorously. "No stress, nothing. I didn't have to get out of the car to walk somewhere. I just stopped by the roadside where the man was standing. When I arrived there, I went to the shoe shop to ask for the man of the house. I was told he was not likely to be in at that time of the day, but when I knocked at the door it was him that received me in, though he was dressed to go out. To me it was God and this is the way the Almighty God has been for me. When I need a favour God always directs me to a person whom He has prepared to grant my request."

The Holy Spirit remains the divine replacement Jesus promised us to help us in fulfilling His purpose. He is described as the Spirit of Witness and Worship. He is the Spirit of Truth and Praise. He is the enabler. He is the Spirit of Christ. He is the custodian of believers. He is the Director-general of kingdom projects, every exploit of faith in Christ on earth that has ever been or will ever be is initiated and perfected by Him. His ministry cannot be overemphasised.

When God gave His Son He gave His best when He gave His Holy Spirit He gave His all.

Anonymous

9

HER PRAYER

As for me, I will call upon God,
And the LORD shall save me.
Evening and morning and at noon
I will pray and cry aloud,
And He shall hear my voice.
Psalm 55:16, 17

It shall come to pass that before they call,
I will answer, and while they are still
Speaking, I will hear.
Isaiah 65:24

"AS a woman of God I do believe your prayer life will be an aspect many will want to know," I told Oluremi Ayida. The efficacy of prayer in the life of a child of God cannot be overemphasised. It is the way of communication with God and also an act of humility acknowledging one's dependence on Him. To this I asked her: "To you Ma, what is prayer all about and can you let us into your prayer life?"

Responding she began: "In my walk with the LORD I have discovered that nothing is too small to pray about. God loves us. He wants us to pray whether it be a big or small thing. He is always there for us to ask. Even I marvel at times over what I pray over, like misplacing a key. I'll be looking for the key and after spending two or three days looking for it then I would just ask myself: "Remi why are you anxious about this key, you haven't prayed about it!" Then I would pray, and after praying I could enter the next room and immediately discover the key. I remember once I was looking for a key and I said, "Well Father, You always want me to pray. Please let me find this key, I don't want to have any anxiety over it." As I stopped praying I just looked down and the key was right where I was standing. "God! You sent Your angel to drop it!" Full of laughter she added, "So, that is our God! He answered immediately."

To Oluremi Ayida some prayers carry instant answers while she also disclosed that some take a longer period of time to be answered. To this she mentioned the attitude of the seeker to be that of perseverance and tenacity, not giving up but reaching the point of answer. Giving an instance she recalls, "My property was seized because it was said that a couple could not own a property each on Victoria Island. When I became a Christian I prayed vehemently to God concerning the injustice. I started attending Holy Ghost nights. When I went to one, a word of knowledge came through the servant of God, "There is a woman here that her property has been seized and God said He has given her back her property." I claimed it thanking and praising God for the word. One day I was reading Psalm one hundred and three in the Bible and when I got to verse six God said, "I will execute judgement and righteousness for those oppressed ..." and then the house came to mind. I said, "God, are you talking to me? That they are oppressing me? That I would get it back?" So I held on to that verse and I started quoting it. Meanwhile they had given some others their properties back, those who had had theirs seized together with mine for the very same reason. I still held on to God's word and that gave me comfort and I was saying it; "God I know You will do it." We were abroad when I learnt that I had received a letter in Nigeria that the Governor had written saying that they had given me back the house. After I claimed the word of knowledge I would have thought that within a short while I would receive a letter returning the property back to me as I had started taking steps concerning the matter. I asked my husband to write to the Governor telling him how wrongly they had treated me but nothing came out of it. I waited for another seven years after that to get my property back. In all it was about twenty-five years that the property was seized. So it all depends on trust and faith. So, for some prayers you receive immediate answers, some it takes years for an answer. God will be waiting to make sure He takes the glory. That is what I have discovered; that no one is sharing the glory with Him. That it's so plain that He did it! That no one can take credit for it, so I've learnt to wait. I've learnt that when I pray, just expect an answer and God can answer it anyway. Even when He doesn't give you that particular request, He does give you something better. He can answer immediately and He can take time but He will answer." *"Pray without ceasing"* (1Thessalonian 5:17) she said.

"I think for any believer serving God in order to succeed you have to pray. And when you pray, God takes over. You are not the one doing it any more. You are just His physical vessel but all other things have been done in the spiritual, as nothing happens in the physical without it happening first in the spiritual and for things to progress, that is, to happen in the spiritual it must be by prayer. The sooner anyone working in the vineyard of God realises that, then the easier the work of God will be for you. Without prayer you cannot get anywhere, as our Lord Jesus Christ, always prayed before His service to His Father. Prayer preceded every miracle He performed. Before He appointed His disciples He went up to a quiet place, separating Himself, praying before coming down to appoint His disciples. In Lazarus's case (John 11:41-42), it was prayer first. So for any success, prayer is very important. This is what I have discovered. We too can accomplish a lot for our God, if we remain close to Him in prayer and obedience. When you do not even get an answer immediately, know that God has a purpose for delaying it. Either because if He had answered it you'll be thinking that it's probably because you did something, or you have worked so hard that immediately you prayed He answered it. *"For by strength no man shall prevail"* (1 Samuel 2:9). He wants to take the glory. What I have discovered is that every delay in answer to my prayer is that God wants the glory. This leaves me with no doubt that when I receive the answer to prayer that this is His doing. There is no two ways about it, no doubt at all. The accident involving my daughter (Her Praise Chapter), He left me with no doubt that He is the one who called me. He said "Pray!" Although I didn't know what would happen. I was praying. Praying in tongues, praying every manner of prayer I knew how to pray."

She spoke as though she was giving a seminar on the subject. I sat listening to her as she spoke out of her wealth of experience. For her personal prayer time Oluremi Ayida revealed that she starts her day praising God after which, she goes to the bathroom and then goes back, separating herself in prayer and reading the Bible. She asks the Holy Spirit, to teach her how to pray and who to pray for. Some of her favourite scriptures amongst others in the place of prayer she says are *Galatians 2:20; Romans 8:28; Isaiah 54:17; Philippians*

4:13; II Timothy 1:7; Isaiah 33:3; II Corinthians 9:12-13; Matthew 11:28-30; 1 John 1:9 and 3 John 2.

Speaking on the family devotional time Oluremi Ayida stated that since the children are no longer under them what she does is that the little time they have together on occasions or holidays she takes it as an opportunity for the entire family to pray together. However with her husband they have a daily devotion together. Affirming this Mr Allison Ayida states: "We have early morning devotion and fellowship. We have a daily reading from the Bible, *Everyday With Jesus*, *The Word for Today* and *Open Heavens* a daily devotional authored by Pastor Adeboye. This is followed by intensive daily prayer, which touches on every member of the family, children, grandchildren, friends and the nation. We all receive the blessings of the Lord."

To Oluremi Ayida prayer is her passion. She said, "I pray over everything, every action. When I am walking on the streets and my attention is drawn to someone, I start praying for the person to come to know God's love and the gift of salvation. When flying on the plane I find myself praying for everyone on the flight. Everyone that comes my way, after greeting them I follow with a 'God bless you.' The Holy Spirit is always prompting me to pray or to fast. Whenever I go on a fast of my own volition it is always a struggle to complete it, but if it is ordained by the Holy Spirit's prompting, I could go on a seven day fast and pray effortlessly. Prayer is my passion and anything that would help me to pray through I go for it. I have seen God answer my prayer immediately or in days or in months or even in years, but He never fails to answer. I pray probably not as much as I should but it is so wonderful that the little I do pray, God is gracious to me."

One can safely conclude that our prayers can lead to real, lasting change, bringing glory to God and great joy to many including ourselves.

We had come to the end of the day's work in her office. It had been a long day, bright and sunny, just a few minutes before five pm. Thanking her for her time I gathered my work, got up and bade her goodbye. I had to make the best use of the time we had today as she was due to travel to the UK at the weekend. Leaving her office I saw that almost every staff had gone. Everywhere was quiet. Mr Godwin had been waiting patiently in the secretary's office. As I walked out seeing him I told him Mummy would need him now to help get her things downstairs as she was set to go. He walked briskly along the corridor to her office while I went out descending the staircase to the ground floor. Pastor Rose and Ms Funmi, members of the staff and Mr Dickson her driver, were there understandably anxious, waiting for her. She emerged from the rear as she had come down using the lift. Coming through the reception and bookshop lounge she walked gently but firmly out of the entrance to her waiting car, being greeted by the rest of us. In no time her car was off the premises.

Without persistence prayers may go unanswered.
Importunity is made up of the ability to hold on, to continue,
to wait with unrelaxed and unrelaxable grasp, restless desire
and restful patience.
E.M. Bounds

10

HER PURSUIT

And He said to them,
Why did you seek Me? Did you not know that
I must be about My Father's business?
Luke 2:49

Jesus said to them,
My food is to do the will of Him who sent Me
and to finish His work.
John 4:34

On a bright, sunny Friday in October at about midday, Oluremi Ayida was set for the afternoon's session. The first we were having since coming back from her overseas trip. As I commented on how much younger she looked, she beamed and softly said, "Thank you". She was dressed in a white cotton collar shirt and a simple scarf tied around her head, as she sat collected in strength on a high-backed chair in her office. We had exchanged pleasantries and it was an interesting atmosphere to get down to work!

Speaking I began:

"Pursuit is the proof of your desire! What you believe in! What you behave! What you belong to!" so I asked Oluremi what her pursuit was.

"My pursuit is that anything I do, I want Christ to be seen in it, to be a light, and to shine for my Lord. Also to influence others, for people to see Christ in me and say, oh we want to follow The Person this person is following; we want to be like her. So many people say: "Oh we want to be like you," and I say, "Well, it is Christ, it is not me." So I just want people to reflect Christ in all that we do, in our relationships, even when we are angry with somebody we should handle it the way Christ would want us to. So my goal in everything is to be Christ-like. That is my primary pursuit."

She spoke with deep conviction in her voice. Thanking her for the initial comments of her own pursuit, I went on further to ask Oluremi Ayida about the things and activities that engage her and what she is involved in that she seeks to pursue every day. This brings me to write briefly of her relentless pursuit of the Kingdom of God. A course to which she gives her time, energy, resource, dedication and commitment. Her untiring pursuit of the kingdom according to God's grace and ability upon her life is reflected in all she has been involved in ever since she came to know the Lord Jesus on a personal note. In her new zeal, Oluremi assumed the headship of the fellowship in 1983 when Mrs Bunmi Adeniji, the pioneer of FBC in Nigeria, handed over to her following her husband's appointment for an international posting by the Federal Government. Before she left for overseas, Mrs Adeniji asked Mrs Oluremi Ayida, Mrs Aby Bucknor and Mrs Bridget Itsueli to go and see Pastor E.A. Adeboye for his fatherly counsel and prayer. Mrs Ayida and Mrs Itsueli turned up for the appointment at the Redeemed Christian Church of God campground to see the servant of God. Pastor Adeboye prayed and laid hands on them confirming their call into the leadership position of the fellowship group. Mrs Ayida was confirmed as the head of the group and Mrs Itsueli as the secretary. At this time it was Mrs Itsueli's house at 2, Mbu Close, S.W. Ikoyi that was used as the fellowship's secretariat.

This takes us through a journey into the Ministry of The WORD and PRAYER (Acts 6:4) known as FRIENDSHIP BIBLE COFFEES (FBC) which has metamorphosed into a larger ministry called FRIENDSHIP BIBLE FELLOWSHIP MINISTRIES (FBFM) an inter-denominational Christian organisation set up to spread the good news of Christ in respective areas which Oluremi Ayida heads as the National Co-ordinator to date. A ministry of impact to lives: individuals, communities and corporations within and outside the country. Oluremi Ayida in her response takes us through the vision of the ministry, its commission and inception and its course so far in Nigeria.

"FBFM is the offshoot of FBC. We started with about six ladies coming together to study the Bible with the help of materials published by StoneCroft Ministries (the International Headquarters of FBC in USA). There is a rule about the growth in that when we are more than twelve in number, we must break and start another group and this has been the pursuit, to make sure that we grow and multiply."

She went on to say that some people get so used to their group that they do not want to break away and start off other groups. "But we cannot grow if we do not multiply, we have to multiply, so this is how we form the groups," she revealed. Interestingly still speaking on the early days of inception she continued, "When we started in my own group we had people coming from Apapa, from Surulere, from Obalende. As we grew we encouraged members coming from these places to start a group in their different areas. In doing this they fix the day and time that suits them. Some areas could be made up of working ladies. In such a case, the study class is fashioned to be in the evening. If they are homemakers like me, the study will be in the morning. So this how we tailor it to suit individual requirements. It is not rigid, we allow for flexibility in time. When a new group starts off in a house in an area, the members commence with the introductory study books. Some studies could last for about twelve weeks; some could be eight weeks or less. However when a member starts a study in a group it is expected that the person should stay in the group until the end of the study. It is possible for a member to be made a 'guide' in another group. The requirement for the guideship position is that the person must be someone who has given their life to Christ, and that Christ is reigning in their lives through the power of the Holy Spirit. A person cannot be a guide if the Holy Spirit is not guiding them because we want people to follow a Godly example and by so doing following Christ," she spoke emphatically.

Continuing to describe the Bible class group Oluremi added, "The lady whose house is being used for the group study is known as the 'Hostess'. She gets the place ready with chairs, table, the attendance register, coffee, tea and biscuits and whether it's the dining room or the sitting room it is made as comfortable as possible. If there aren't any chairs, we don't even mind sitting on the floor," she spoke enthusiastically, painting a picture of how a group could be, with her words. The air of readiness, thirst in the souls of attending members and the joy of being together with a common goal of coming to learn at the 'Master's feet', was the imagination one could visibly see as she spoke. Recounting one of their classes, Mrs Oluremi Ayida says, "We've been to a house that we sat on the floor. The lady had just moved and she said she wanted us to come. She didn't have a dining table or chairs yet, so we all sat round. Thank God, we were not old then," she humorously added meeting with a gentle laugh from us both. "This is FBC and this is how we've been going. People will come and when they eventually move or get transferred to somewhere else we still continue to encourage them. We encourage them to become guides so that they can start other groups in their new location. There is a 'co-ordinator,' somebody that will oversee to the smooth running of the groups in an area. The co-ordinator has the responsibility of supplying the study books and other relevant materials from the office and collecting love offerings from members at the end of every study book which goes towards the cost of printing."

I prompted. The course of FBC/FBFM in Nigeria in relation to men, machinery, materials, money and motion is profound. It reveals a practical picture of the parable of the small mustard seed told by our Lord Jesus. It started as a little seed, which has grown into a tree useful and beneficial to its environment.

To this, Mrs Oluremi Ayida interjected that it was through the Friendship Bible Coffees (FBC) study groups that Friendship Bible Fellowship Ministries evolved. She reflects, then tells me that through the weekly studies, she was so hungry and so thirsty for the word of God that she could not rest but wanted something to do everyday. It was through this longing that she came across the *Every Day with Jesus* publication. In registering the ministry, the name: Friendship Bible Coffees could not be used because as she said the word 'Coffees' was alien to the Nigerian culture. She explains, "We don't often drink coffee, we drink tea. People were not taking us seriously with the name, because they associated the getting together of women over coffee to be gossip. We then prayed and asked God for a suitable name and He gave us 'Friendship Bible Fellowship Ministries' because we are all friends."

The registered ministry's name became a larger umbrella under which other arms of the ministry began. Different members were given inspiration from God to start off these features of the ministry. For example, the Children's Holiday Camp was handed over to the person who received the vision for it. It became her 'baby' under her charge and nurture. The same was for the Youth Club, Prayer Cells, Outreaches and Seminars, Bible College, distribution of Christian literature, Christian Counselling – which is a new addition, and of course the Bible Study Groups. On the features of the FBFM, Oluremi Ayida went further to give a detailed account of the purpose and activities involved for each department.

For the FBC, the foundation scripture is *"and ye shall know the truth…"* (John 8:32). FBC is a home Bible study, the aim being for the participants to live a Christ-like life in the community. She gave three reasons why FBC is a must for everyone. The first, being that the class is exciting! Because people who study the Bible discover its relevance to life every day, and if its teaching is applied to their daily living they will find answers to life's problems. Secondly, they are different! They are small groups meeting in homes, having 'guides' instead of teachers. They have discussions instead of lectures and the studies are short courses varying in length from 5–14 weeks. Lastly they are for everyone! Men, women, young people of all ages from all faiths and all walks of life where neighbours meet informally to read and discuss the world's Greatest book 'THE BIBLE.'

The scripture; *"pray without ceasing"* (1 Thessalonians 5:17) is the basis of the prayer cells. Prayer advisors or prayer leaders in homes conduct these. In this group, people meet to pray, learn to pray by praying, reading the Word of God and worshipping God in 'spirit and in truth.' It is also a time when members intercede in prayer for the nation, churches and for urgent needs of members. The meeting should not last more than one and half-hours.

The biblical injunction: *"train up a child in the way he should go…"* (Proverbs 22: 6) is the premise for the FBFM's Children's Holiday Camp. It is an outreach programme where children experience an exciting three weeks packed with interesting and stimulating activities. It is intended to bring the best out of the children so that the Word of God would indwell them from an early age. The camp is staffed with well-educated Christian mothers who volunteer their time from 10 am to 3 pm every weekday; the mothers are assisted by paid Christian staff. The camp's curriculum includes daily Bible reading, discussion time, computer, English, French and mathematics lessons. The children are also given art lessons, drama, calligraphy (writing) and a well-equipped children's library is provided where children are encouraged to spend time reading quietly, supervised by library attendants. Their outdoor activities include tennis instructions, basketball, football, handball and gymnastics. Every Friday there is an end of week social where meals are shared and also a party for the birthday babies of the month.

"Wherewithal shall a young man cleanse his way? By taking heed thereto according to thy word." (Psalm 119: 9) forms the underlying word for the FBFM Youth Club. Its aim is to reach out to fellow youths to share the 'Good news' of our Lord and Saviour Jesus Christ with them. The activities of the club include:

1. Bible study, which involves the studying of God's Word so as to make the Word true to daily living.

2. Annual youth camp – meeting during the long vacation.

3. Outreaches through retreats, birthday fellowship parties, picnics etc.

4. Music and drama group

5. Counselling sessions by seasoned Christians / career counsellors to counsel youths on the choice of professions and good Christian living.

6. Pen ministry – where youths who are talented in journalism and writing are encouraged to lift Jesus' Name high through the writing of articles in newsletters and magazines and through letter writing to friends.

7. Prayer ministry, where the youths offer intercessory prayers for the growth of their club, the nation and churches throughout the world.

8. Workshops, where arts and crafts sessions are organised and for which exhibitions of products, paintings, drawings, weaving, cookery, etc. are made.

The growth of the ministry has been steady over the years. Starting with just one group, it now has over 100 groups in Lagos, more than 200 groups in Port Harcourt, 4 groups in Abuja, 4 groups in Ijebu and one in Warri. As Oluremi Ayida speaks of the growth of the ministry, "When FBC started, Pentecostals churches were few then. The ministry at this became an avenue where people's appetite for the word of God was cultured and watered. However with the increase of Pentecostal churches, our members started joining the churches where they became more committed, thereby not having enough time to attend the FBC classes. Many members are now Pastors, Deacons in these churches," she recalled enthusiastically.

FBC now became like a channel that launched members to greater heights. She mentioned Tony Rapu, a well known preacher of God's Word and Pastor in Nigeria who started as a member with the Friendship Bible Coffees and became a guide. From there he joined the Redeemed Christian Church of God after hearing Pastor Adeboye at a meeting he had with the FBC. He rose to become a Pastor in the church and was used by God to enhance the spiritual and numerical growth of youths in the church.

A lot of ladies from the ministry she said are now Pastors, Evangelists in one place or the other. Ms Funto Babalola who was from the Surulere FBC group is now a Pastor. Mrs Okoro founded and now heads a church. Also another member Mr Remi Kilo who was also sponsored by the ministry and recently graduated as a minister from the Anglican Theological College, is now a curate in one of the rural areas in Nigeria. All these are examples Mrs Ayida gave in describing how God had used the ministry to nurture, train and release people into their divine purposes as she recalled with a sense of fulfilment. She puts it, "It gladdens my heart to see that they are growing and nurturing others because I can't keep them."

The growth of the FBFM has increased over the years in vision and direction by the Holy Spirit. According to Oluremi Ayida, basically the vision of the Ministry under her leadership is knowing God through His Word. She mentioned that the features of the Ministry which amongst others includes the FBC Bible study, publication and distribution of Christian literature, are aimed at helping many to know Christ and for the Body of Christ to grow by the Word. This she said is the mandate of the ministry. She says, "Every time God speaks, He says, 'I just want you to encourage people to read My Word.'" She continued, "In whatever way we can reach them for the Lord. We also started with the children. The Bible says teach your children the way of the Lord and when he is old he will not depart from it. So we followed that scripture and we started the Children's Holiday Camp, that is, 'catching them young.' As the children attended the Camp they began to ask their parents such questions like: 'Mummy, why don't we pray before eating?' Or, 'Why don't you allow us to go to Sunday school?' Through the camp some of the mothers have become our partners – helping the ministry financially or materially. A mother even bought the Camp a T.V. when we needed one!"

The ministry also holds regular Christian Seminars and Outreaches where men of God within and outside the country are invited to give talks and to minister to people. She mentioned amongst others

Ministries in America while she was in Geneva, Mrs Adeniji came back to Nigeria with this seed of God's Word. In no time the fellowship started in April 1982 with six ladies namely Mrs Esther Nanna, Mrs Bunmi Adeniji, Mrs Remi Ayida, Mrs Abby Bucknor, Mrs Janet Ohiwerei and the late Chief (Mrs) Hilda Ogunbanjo. Over time, the FBC has grown into a large active and dynamic ministry of committed Christians with several groups in many parts of Lagos and other states in Nigeria. The FBFM ministry is also responsible for printing the FBC study books by kind permission of StoneCroft ministry. She joyfully shares "FBC studies have indeed changed my whole life. It has caused me to turn my whole life to Jesus Christ when I invited Him to come into my life. The study has made me answer the call of God to serve Him. FBC have changed the lives of many men and women in Nigeria. God is using FBC to draw many souls to His Kingdom. FBC is a wonderful tool God has given the world to reach people and turn them to Him, to God be the glory!"

The readership and distribution range of *Every Day with Jesus* bi-monthly publications also continues to increase in Nigeria, though not without challenges, such as pirating and stealing at the beginning. However the printers, Academy Press did everything possible to surmount this both internally and externally. Adequate supervision and special security was put in place to ensure that the delivery and distribution ran smoother. To this Oluremi Ayida also added that prayer played an important role to achieving this success. Asked how many registered Distributors there are now, she reflects, "We have more than a hundred in various states." However she said some of the distributors, after taking their orders do not meet up to bring back the returns on the sales. The ministry does sometimes give incentive to motivate the distributors by allowing a 30-day period for payment. The National Co-ordinator indicated that the ministry had lost a lot of money from distributors, which they could hardly reach in some states. She says the ministry continues to pray for honest distributors for improvement in the network.

As the head of the ministry authorised to print and distribute EDWJ Oluremi Ayida says:

"For the printing, we pay royalty. CWR allow us to print here but we pay royalty per copy to them to cover part of the overhead costs." Having spoken extensively on the vision and operations of the Friendship Bible Fellowship ministries, where Oluremi Ayida spends a very significant part of her time and life in pursuit of divine assignment, I couldn't help but present her with some barrage of questions on her personal life in relation to the office she occupies. Looking at Oluremi Ayida's physique now and the full force of her vigorous life at this age, I asked her how she coped in terms of physical and moral energy of strength to continue her work properly?

As the National Co-ordinator of an International ministry, coupled with other activities of home, church, community I asked Oluremi if after her overcharged day was over, she found it difficult to relax, to sleep. "Do you read? Take pills? or lie, brooding over problems? Won't you tell me about some of the smaller details of your life and work? The things you do and like to do; your daily time table and particular way of relaxing?" I knew I had given her a lot of things to think and talk about at the same time. I wanted to be as practical and real as possible. I knew she was up to it. She is willing to share her life with others. Not as though she is a 'super human being' but having the strength that comes from acknowledging and accepting one's human weaknesses, frailties and inadequacies for God's own strength, might and ability for living.

She paused, reflects and then began to speak in a soft gentle tone. "Well, I start my day between five and six am, mostly five am. I would go to a quiet place in the house and have my own personal time with the Lord. Soon after my husband would join me for our family devotion, where our Bible reading is followed with exhortation and prayers."

"I'm not a breakfast person but as I'm getting older, I try to have a light breakfast, like a piece of toast, a glass of orange juice and a cup of tea. I wouldn't have breakfast until I'd finished praying. When I am waiting on the Lord I break my fast at two pm. Whatever I do, I try to have at least two meals a day, my favourite food is well made Jollof rice," she revealed.

Oluremi Ayida says her day is always engaged with diverse activities as the Lord leads her. According to her, "I've got so many children now. All of FBC members are my children." Sometimes she is very much involved at different occasions and sometimes plays supportive roles. Sometimes she has to support ministries and churches by her physical attendance at special programmes. Her involvement in marriage counselling sessions at her local church, Our Saviour's Church, and the initial Introductory classes for churches wanting to adopt the FBC studies into their programmes forms part of her regular activities.

"God has been so good to me," she said as she advanced to answer earlier questions. "Like I once mentioned, when I work so hard especially when we're having seminars or other activities, I get so tired and wonder if I can face the following day. By the time I wake up in the morning, it's as if nothing happened the day before. I'm refreshed and energised. I don't even know where it comes from but I know it is the Lord. I sleep well but sometimes the Holy Spirit would wake me up and something would come to my mind. I sometimes put down my thoughts and ask the Holy Spirit to help me put my thoughts and plans to action and invariably the Lord would direct me on how to do it."

What about taking pills for sleeping or relaxing? I prompted trying to help bring back the questions to light. "No, no, I don't take pills, " she said with a higher lilt to her voice. "That was before when I was in the world, to sleep I would take Valium. I was almost addicted to Valium as I used to suffer from migraines. Even if I'm going out to speak to just two people, I would have to take Valium, but no more, no Valium or any other sedative. Nothing! Christ is my Valium!" she answered bursting out in laughter of which I simultaneously took part.

On how she really relaxes I asked do you have personal activities that you like to do, like tidying, sorting out your wardrobe, going through photograph albums? Or do you like fashion? Or is it when the children or grandchildren come around?

Still in a humorous note, Oluremi says, "I like a tidy surrounding. So I'm always tidying things in one place or the other. Sometimes I tidy so much that I don't even know where I've kept some of my things. I love having my grandchildren around me! It gives me joy when they come. I always do read. I read Christian books and newspapers. Before, I used to read fashion magazines, novels and romance stories. But now I rather read something spiritual to refresh my mind." One of the books she has appreciated reading recently is, *The Foolishness of God*, by Dr Femi Aribisala. She said the book gave her a better understanding of the workings of God. What seemed foolish to the natural senses of men might just be what The Spirit of God uses to reveal His power and wisdom over man's limitations. (1 Corinthians 1:25-29).

What have you got to say about your fashion sense? How do you choose your clothes? I asked her. She laughed, "Well, I'm very particular and mindful about how I dress now that I am a Christian. Before I became a Christian I liked to make impressions. I liked it when heads turned as I appeared at a gathering. I remembered one of my daughters, the one that is a Doctor, said that she wanted to be a nurse. I asked her why she wanted to be one. Her reason was that she wanted to wear the nice uniforms I wore because back then I got my uniforms from America ready made. I wore a uniform a day, all nicely starched and looking smart. I was always like that, but all that was vanity, nothing but vanity. However I've come to a stage where I ask the Holy Spirit to choose what to wear and how to tie my headgear. The Holy Spirit has become my best friend and partner in everything I do. Now I want to look good for God and not for man. I say, "I want to look good for You," she spoke humorously with bursts of laughter. I prompted saying, "And for Daddy too!" (Referring to her husband). There was much laughter at this as she chorused, "Yes! For Big Daddy and small Daddy!" Oluremi had this to add, "I don't paint my nails, I don't wear lipstick, now everything is done in moderation."

Every age has its own tempo and lifestyle: but in each age there are always those who care deeply for things of the Spirit and carry the love of their fellow men and all humanity with them, throughout their lives. In this respect they belong to all ages and are universal as the centuries go by.

An accomplished woman of character and purpose, an icon, a successful leader, a mentor, humble, selfless, caring and compassionate. A woman of dignity, a General in God's army who has the ability of identifying talents and gifts among her colleagues and membership and encouraging them to grow and mature to the expansion of Christ's kingdom on earth and the benefit of humanity. Standing at the heart of the progressive surge of God's work on earth at different levels, Oluremi Victoria Ayida is this person. She has travelled around the globe in answer to God's calling on her life and many hundreds of people have come to know Christ personally as a direct result of her ministry.

The FBC / FBFM has been a movement and not a monument in Nigeria. It is by the power of the Spirit of God, that progression has taken place in the ministry's activities and projects in Nigeria in the advancement of the kingdom of our Lord Jesus Christ. The Ministry duly registered as a non-profit making Christian organisation has at its helm of affairs notable and well respected Nigerian citizens, who have proven character and integrity as they continue in their Christian walk.

Mr Felix Ohiwerei serves as the Chairman, Board of Directors for the FBFM. The Board members are: Mrs Remi Ayida, Dr (Mrs) Cecilia Ibru, Mr Felix Ohiwerei, Mrs Bridget Itsueli, Mrs Omoniyi Olowokande, Mrs Ebun Onabanjo, Mr Samuel Yilu, Mrs Nkiru Green, Mrs H.E. Coker, Mrs A. Ukiwe and Mrs Victoria Majekodunmi.

The FBFM has as her Trustees: Olorogun Michael Ibru, Dr Imo Itsueli, Mrs Bridget Itsueli and Mrs Remi Ayida.

It has no doubt been a consistent, concentrated and concerted effort and commitment of teamwork in the ministry as a whole. FBFM has a great hope and a great future because men and women, old and young from all walks of life have been willing to give their lives that God be glorified. To God alone be the glory for the great things He has done! And He is doing, as it is usually sung in the Ministry's Anthem:

For I'm building a people of power
And I'm making a people of praise,
That will move thro' this land by My Spirit,
And will glorify My precious Name.

And as His people chorus in affirmation:

Build Your Church, Lord,
Make us strong, Lord,
Join our hearts, Lord, through Your Son
Make us one, Lord, in Your Body
In the Kingdom of Your Son.

Fondly called "Mummy" by many, Oluremi Ayida's role as the National Co-ordinator of these kingdom activities, projects and investments in the ministry since inception has been the release of God's functional grace upon her life manifest from strength to strength, faith to faith and glory to glory!

I slept and dreamt
That life was joy
I awoke and saw
That life was duty
I acted, and behold
Duty was joy.
– Rabindranath Tagore

11

HER PROGRESS

For exaltation comes neither from the east
Nor from the west nor from the south.
Psalm 75: 6

Then He said to them all,
If anyone desires to come after Me, let him
deny himself,
and take up his cross daily, and follow Me.
Luke 9: 23

God is and remains a God of progress. He activates, kick starts and sustains the process of progression, which differs from person to person in all aspects of life. The Bible in describing the Body of Christ calls children of God lively stones, parts of the body fitly joined together, each complementing the role or activity of the other and working towards a common goal in the kingdom. There is no competition but a complementing, no breaking of ranks but an advancement, a forward movement in kingdom exploits according to the several abilities and grace bestowed upon each by the Spirit of God and all working to His glory. As God's people we are expected to be faithful over the number of talents given to us, trading with it, gaining more, making returns on God's investment.

His lord said unto him, well done, thou good and faithful
servant: thou hast been faithful over a few things, I will make
thee ruler over many things; enter thou into the joy of thy lord ...
Matthew 25:21

For Oluremi Ayida it has been a progressive life of imparting and impacting lives around her. She has made progress in her upward and inward relationship with her Lord and Saviour as well as her downward and outward relationship with fellow man in diverse respects by the grace of God.

It was in London, early in the year, 2005. I got a phone call from the National co-ordinator of the Friendship Bible Fellowship Ministries, Nigeria. She was around for a short visit. I concluded on an appointment to see her for a session of discussions with her. It was a cold and icy Thursday morning. I arrived at the Ayida's residence about half an hour behind schedule. It had taken a little while in locating the house somewhere in north west London. I walked through the front gate down the path that led to the entrance of the house. I enjoyed the serenity that the garden offered. I noticed the lushness of the green trees and shrubs that stood on both sides of the entrance looking well trimmed. They were wet with the frost that had fallen on them. Already being expected, the door opened as I pressed the bell. I walked into an adjacent sitting room where her husband and two of their grandchildren, Kome and her sister, Efena, warmly welcomed me as they sat watching the television. In a little while Oluremi Ayida tenderly but gracefully descended the staircase into the room where we were. She was wearing a deep pink turtle neck top over black trousers and a soft cushioned slippers on her feet. Her hair was neat and trimmed short. I stood up. Taking a little step towards her, I greeted her in the usual custom of kneeling half way. She responded excitingly as she ushered me into an impressively beautiful and tasteful inner living room where we did a full day's work.

I asked Oluremi Ayida to describe the progress she has made so far in various aspects of her life.

Speaking she recalled the time, when she was a part of a Bible Study class in Mrs Adeniji's house in Ikoyi. They were studying the third lesson in the book of Mark. The class turned out to be exactly what she had wanted. From that time, she began to attend the study once a week. It marked the beginning of a new life for her in Christ. The hostess, Mrs Adeniji, shortly after sometime told her that she would also start another group in her house at the end of the study book. At first she was frightened at the 'call' but she put it before the Lord in prayer. In a short while, a new class commenced in Oluremi Ayida's house. "I started by just being part of a group of six people studying the Bible together once a week and I really enjoyed it very much. I was so hungry for the word of God that I didn't want it to be just once a week. I wanted to be a daily study but it was not possible. Then I said, 'God, if only You can give me something so that I could have fellowship with you every day.'"

On one of her trips to England to see her children when they had their school half term, she worshipped at All Souls Church in Langham Place, W.1. At the end of the service she took a visit to their bookstore where she discovered *Every Day with Jesus*. Picking up a copy she bought, she read it and enjoyed it. At the end of one week Oluremi said she went back and bought four extra copies to take to Nigeria. "I gave one copy to my sister and one to Mrs Adeniji and to two other people. So I had something doing everyday which came as an answer to my prayer. Not only did I enjoy it, I started wanting other people to enjoy reading it as well by having a daily fellowship with the Lord. Then I started making copies from my own copy. Everytime I visited London, I brought back a few copies of it and then I photocopied a lot for distribution to friends and FBC members, so the copies were increasing among the members."

The copies were being given out free to members. Later on it was so much they had to start selling at a cost to cover the stationery expenses. "The distribution grew so much but along the line the Holy Spirit ministered that what we were doing was not right. It was wrong for us to be making copies of what we didn't have the permission to do. So at the Bible Study I told the group about it and suggested that we should write to the author and request if copies of the devotional could be sent per time to sell in Nigeria." After much deliberation among members, a letter was prayerfully written to the author of *Every Day with Jesus*. In a short while a reply came inviting the group to come to England to have a meeting with them. Oluremi Ayida said that she was not in London then, so she suggested that Mrs Bridget Itsueli, who is the secretary of FBC working committee and who wrote the letter and was still in London should attend. She asked her to go in company of any other member of FBC in London then. She got Mrs Cecilia Ibru and Mrs Comfort Hayes. Rev. Selwyn Hughes suggested to them at the meeting that FBC should be registered as a ministry and that they should draw up a feasibility study to see if there is a market for a Bible reading aid and the possibility of the publication being printed in Nigeria. She said the group could not afford the cost of the feasibility study at that time even though they got a company to do it. Dr Imo Itsueli decided to pay for the cost on behalf of the group. The company that took up the study however were so blessed with the devotional that they waived the cost of the feasibility study as their own contribution to the inroad of the devotional in Nigeria.

After concluding on the feasibility study, a second interview was held in England in 1989. It was attended by Dr & Mrs Itsueli and Mrs Ayida, where they had discussions with Trevor Partridge and David Rivett, the Directors of Crusade for World Revival (CWR) concerning the study. It was agreed upon that copies of *Every Day with Jesus* would be sent from England to the fellowship in Nigeria bi-monthly to sell because they had not yet been given permission to begin printing in Nigeria. They started by sending a thousand copies while the author, Rev. Selwyn Hughes promised to visit Nigeria and to give permission to print when the sale gets to ten thousand. So in 1990 they started sending 1,000 copies, which were being sold among the members and to the Nigerian public at large. They were also told not to pay, that is, not to make returns on sale, rather the fellowship was advised to open a bank account where the money should be saved and would go a long way in helping to promote his coming to Nigeria.

This development necessitated the formal and official registration of the ministry at the advice of the author. The next order went up to between 3,000 to 4,000. By 1991, the order had reached 10,000 copies. Precisely by July/August the ministry had started to receive these number of copies. It was however so difficult getting them through the import customs in Nigeria, and a lot of money had to be paid for this. The ministry at this time wrote officially to the author informing of the increase in copies distributed and he replied that he would be in Nigeria for his first visit in November 1991. Oluremi Ayida speaking says:

"When he came he had a seminar, a Christian counselling for ministers, church leaders and workers; and a marriage seminar. The Lord helped me to pick Pastors Austen Ukachi and Wale Adefarasin, Dr Tony Rapu, Mr Yemi Akinsanya, a lawyer with Mobil Oil of Nigeria, Rev. Yinka Omololu from the Anglican Communion and some FBC members who formed the planning committee for the visit and to co-ordinate the programme. We had units such as the prayer, publicity, planning and protocol that were responsible for different duties. The venue of the programme was the University of Lagos Auditorium. The hall was packed full, people came from all over Nigeria and the FBC had to organise for accommodation of some guests. It was a success. God really promoted the programme."
She continued as she recalled the stages of progress that have taken

place in the ministry over the years, which has not been without its 'ups and downs.'

"The marriage seminar was very successful. A couple who had separated for many years came to that seminar and they reconciled there. Letters were written to me speaking of the effect of the seminar in their lives. And at the end of that visit, the next *Every Day with Jesus* we ordered was about 16,000. So that was how it jumped to almost double as people were asking for more of the devotionals. That's progress!"

For the FBC Study groups, there was also a simultaneous progress at the emergence of EDWJ in Nigeria. People were coming to the study groups. The publications and the seminars were being used as a forum to introduce the Friendship Bible Coffees Studies to people and to invite them to be a part of it. People even from outside Lagos who attended the seminars were starting FBC groups in their own places. She went on, "From then we started growing more and more, people started demanding and writing to Rev. Hughes to come to Nigeria. Since then he has been coming. His first visit was only to Lagos. His visit to Owerri was a big success. People were coming out with their fetish things from their homes surrendering them and burning them, it was very successful. Port Harcourt was a success too! We were highly honoured to welcome Selwyn back in 2001 for his fourth visit. The visit was a memorable one as he ministered in Abuja. With every visit there was always a programme in Lagos. For every visit we had an increase in the number of people coming to the evening rallies and seminars. Concentration was on training ministers and leaders and in teachings on the art of Christian counselling. Then they started adding seminars for women and also a forum for professional women for topics such as 'How to be a secure woman' and 'Marriage as God intended.' From there we've been growing gradually. Along with EDWJ we started adding his books like *Cover to Cover* a 365 day Bible reading aid and many other publications on counselling. We have been given approval not only to print EDWJ but also some of his other books in Nigeria. We've added the children's books: '*TOPZ*' - a daily devotional for children aged 7-11, '*YPS*' – EDWJ for youths aged 12-18, and *Inspiring Women Every Day* (IWED). More recently we have introduced to the market a large print of EDWJ to help the elderly with impaired sight. We are expecting the team from Waverley Abbey to come to Nigeria sometime in 2006 for a women's seminar."

With a soft tone that seemed to express thankfulness and accomplishment as she gave the progress report of the ministry so far, Oluremi Ayida continued. "Our distribution before was mainly in Lagos but now we also have it in Kaduna, Kano, Minna, Jos, Jigawa, Zaria, Onitsha, Port Harcourt. Places where we've never even heard of, we now have EDWJ reaching there including the south. The north is very difficult to penetrate but as God would have it our agents in Kaduna and Zaria are distributing over 2000 copies each and our agent in Abuja about 5000 copies, so we have made progress."

She described the rate of public awareness of the devotional in Nigeria as having increased saying many people in the Christendom now make use of it. Oluremi said that in her early years she was not aware of devotionals except for the 'Daily Bread' by the Scripture Union. She also talked about the progress in the location of the ministry from the initial stage, saying, "when we started in my house, we grew to the point that we needed another place. There wasn't any more room in my house to use. A member then gave us a four bedroom flat, which we used for FBC and were also given a place at Prince's Court, which we used for EDWJ. We were growing so much we started putting money aside for our permanent site. Even now the building is getting too small!"

At this, laughing, I said, "The building at Akoka? That's wonderful!" It was amazingly exciting to hear that the three storey building that houses the ministry's headquarters erected a few years back was already getting too small for her operations.

"Yes! Yes!" at Akoka, Oluremi prompted with confidence in her voice, nodding her head to affirm her statement. Initially the books were not so much compared to the space at the new building. Now the volume of books for the various sections has increased greatly over time. Recently a modern lift has been constructed in the building not only to facilitate the movement of the older staff and members but also to help take the cartons of books to the big room upstairs. This has lessened the congestion downstairs.

According to Oluremi, the construction of the lift has been another stride of progress the ministry has made. It was dedicated for operations in the last quarter of year 2004 after one of the regular Thursday lunch hour fellowship by Pastor Samuel Yilu of the Mountain of Fire and Miracles Ministries with the leadership and staff in attendance.

The mention of Pastor Yilu brought Mrs Ayida to say that, "He was a member of FBC and now he has become a Pastor, like I said earlier about Tony Rapu. A lot of our 'girls' like Mrs Green is now a Deaconess in the Redeemed Church; Mrs Omatsone has become a Pastor with the Four Square Church. So that is the progress of what God has started, so small but He's using it to expand His kingdom, to Him be the glory!"

Going on about the progress of the ministry, the Christmas evangelistic outreach held in different parts of the city recorded an increase to 15 meetings in 2004. It is expected that the number will double for the next year. Oluremi Ayida added that someone has given the ministry three acres of land. The ministry is already nurturing the vision of an Old People's Home, a permanent children's holiday camp, and other facilities in the future.

Personally Oluremi Ayida has been given a number of recognition by different bodies and organisations on state and national levels in the country. These have been landmarks of progress in her life. The Dominican Fathers and Brothers Society Award for vocational supports (Catholic Church Organisation) was given in 1985. In December 2003, the National Council of Women Societies Lagos State branch gave her a millennium award in appreciation of immense input in the empowerment of women. On the 14th December 2004 she received recognition for outstanding service to humanity from the National Council of Nigerian Women Society in Abuja which is a part of the International Council of Women (ICW). The Lagos Anglican Diocese Care Ministry Honour Award was given to Oluremi Ayida in July 2004 for tremendous support and selfless service to the elders. In June 2005 she received a Women's Achievers Award from the Women's wing of the Christian Association of Nigeria (CAN), Lagos state branch.

Asked the essence of these Awards and on the platform for which she was given, Oluremi Ayida responded, "God has used the FBFM to reach out to the lives of women in Lagos State and in Nigeria as a whole. Women, who have been anxious over their children and women whose marriages were falling apart have had succour. When they come to Bible study classes, they have God ministering to them and they receive comfort. Consequently their attitudes begin to change because the essence of FBC is to change lives through God's Word thereby changing attitudes at home and in the community. This has really done a lot and has profited many rather than women just going to parties, buying aso-ebi (uniformed attire). They have seen how God is transforming lives through this ministry. I think that there is beginning to be an awareness, recognition of people when they are affecting lives through the work in God's vineyard."

Also in February 2004 a Pentecostal church, 'He's Alive Chapel' (Women Alive) honoured her with an award for Service and Faithfulness. The justification for honouring men and women that have served the Lord with passion, love, commitment and with their substance according to the leadership of the church is taken from the first book of Timothy, the seventeenth verse of the fifth chapter and the first Thessalonican Epistle, the twelfth and thirteenth verses also of the fifth chapter.

Let the elders that rule well be counted worthy of double honour,
especially they who labour in the word and doctrine.

And we beseech you brethren,
to know them which labour among you,
and are over you in the Lord, and admonish you;
And to esteem them very highly in love for their work's sake.
And be at peace among yourselves.

At this commendation service Oluremi Ayida responded, "Jesus has honoured Himself through me and not only me, but also every member of FBC. He's the One doing the work," she spoke with a sense of awe and worship as she concluded with the hymn: 'To God be the Glory, great things He has done ...'

Oluremi Ayida made reference to President Obasanjo's remark when he was incarcerated. "He encouraged us that we should continue to extend our service to the prisons, so since then we have been sending *Every Day with Jesus* to them. That testimony has motivated us to start the Prison Ministry."

At this point I recalled a testimony which a woman gave at the commendation service at He's Alive chapel. She was healed of every trace of a diagnosed sickness after reading the EDWJ devotional teaching on the book of Job in 1991. Perhaps the distribution of the devotionals should also be extended to hospitals in the country in the near future.

In the last quarter of year 2004, Oluremi Ayida was also nominated as a member of 'The Gideonites', (affiliated to the

Redeemed Christian Church of God), a handful of people who are committed to giving financially to the work of God. Coming home to her local assembly she said, "I've been a member of the Parish Council thrice now. The first time when it was under the colonial government when we had Rev. Payne and twice when the church was taken over under the Nigerian Anglican Communion. In the church I have encouraged them to start a pre-marriage counselling ministry which we are running and we are using the FBC study book: *Christ in the home*. Not only in my church but also in other churches we encourage members to approach their church leaders to see if this will also be encouraged and many of them have been using it. They've found it very helpful and young couples too have testified to it in their lives. And what we do now even after the marriage, we try to bring the couples back to have a seminar with them on: *Communication in the Home* which is another book of ours."

Oluremi Ayida in her focus to Christian service a few years back was also co-opted to be a member of the Board of Elderly Help line of the Anglican Communion of Nigeria (Lagos Diocese). The activity of this group help the elderly meet regularly to have fellowship together in various ways with the FBC study books also being adopted. The FBC studies have received much recognition and acceptance to them that they now have the discussed studies on audio tapes to facilitate its use even in their homes. For the privilege of some elderly members, the StoneCroft ministries in America have given approval to the Anglican church to translate the study books into Yoruba, the tribal language of the western part of the country, and the FBC study book on *Living my new life* is already in the process of translation. In the near future it is expected that the studies would also be translated into Igbo and Hausa to meet the needs of some people in the eastern and northern parts of the country respectively.

For Oluremi Ayida her 'walk of faith' over the years back has culminated into progress made in diverse aspects of life. Though not without the training, trials and tests of faith that attends with it also, this Handmaiden of God continues to forge ahead in the strength of the One in whom she has come to put her trust in. She is learning that faith is an attitude of an abiding confidence. It is positive expectation, which mandates preparation. The wisest man that ever lived in one of the three thousand proverbs he spoke says:

The preparation (readiness) of the heart in man, and the answer
(result) of the tongue, is from the LORD.

Frank Tyger's statement: "Progress is not created by contented people" is a popular saying, it is not contradictory to the scripture where it says, "*... godliness with contentment is great gain.*" (1 Timothy 6:6)

Contentment does not necessarily mean a lack of ambition or vision but the acknowledgement of a restful satisfaction and confidence of God's workings in the lives of His people. Its tranquillity is the apex of existence.

I humbly asked Oluremi in a candid session of interview to let us in into personal things she does to enhance her progress and the role she plays. She puts it; "Since I gave my life to Christ I love reading Christian books and testimonies from other people. I also appreciate attending seminars, conventions, like the one held by the Redeemed Christian Church. I've also attended a number of conferences at the StoneCroft Ministries. If a man of God is having a crusade and it is impressed in me to attend, I want to be there as that is how I grow in faith. Like I said earlier on I would always invite friends to go with me and I have taken great pleasure in also seeing them grow." "Partnership and liberality in the spirit one might say!" I exclaimed.

A wise man will hear, and will increase learning
and a man of understanding shall attain unto wise counsels.
(Proverbs 1:5)

She went on, "I also learn from members in the ministry. When I see a member progressing spiritually and I see Christ in them I want to know what they are doing that I am not doing. I thirst for more. For instance it was from a member that I heard of 'Vigils'. I had never heard of it until I started FBC and since then I've started having vigils and God has really used it to bless my life and the ministry."

Sometimes, we as humans learn from the mistakes we make. They have a way of bringing us to humility before God and sometimes before men. It becomes a hindsight, which plays a helpful role of learning in our foresight and insight of issues and in decision making.

Answering to the question I asked her about learning from her mistakes, Oluremi Ayida says: "When I make a mistake I try not to dwell on it for too long. I try to mend my ways. I learn from it and move on and try not to repeat what caused it. I ask God to show me the right way and help me to follow it. For example, I have discovered that when we are having outreaches, the outreach that is successful is the one we spend more time praying about. So I don't allow anything to stop me from praying when I have something important to do. I spend more time to pray, I even have vigils. Whenever Selwyn Hughes is coming we have vigils and we see the results. Since we commenced praying in-house for the ministry, we have been meeting up every morning before the day's work to pray. We also meet once a month for a longer time of prayer. We have seen results because of the prayers we have made. So nothing will make me stop that because I know when we are not praying we are not progressing. This is the essence of having a 'Powerhouse' at the topmost floor of the building. It is a place where people spend time to go before God in prayer. The ministry belongs to the Lord so communication with Him is important for progress," she said with a strong tone of conviction that progress has a correlation with prayer. It again brings to light Paul's words in the Philippian Epistle in the thirteenth and fourteenth verses of the third chapter.

Brethren, I count not myself to have apprehended; but this one thing I do, forgetting those things which are behind, and reaching forth unto those which are before, I press toward the mark for the prize of the high calling of God in Christ Jesus.

The Virtuous woman described in the thirty-first chapter of Proverbs has her husband as one who is known at the gates, because he sits among the elders of the land being an elder himself. Suffice it to say that he occupies an important position in decision making of his immediate and extended environment. To coin it up: "He matters where it matters." For her children alike: *"they arise up and call her blessed ..."* having now being fulfilled in their own lives and acknowledging the labour of their mother upon their lives as the grace of God.

I asked Oluremi Ayida of the progress she has made in her family life over the years gone by. It is a well-known saying that 'charity begins at home.'

"I thank God for progress in raising up the children. Before I met Christ, I thought it was by my effort that I could raise them as I used to be anxious and worry over them all the time. How I wished

I were a true Christian when I was raising my children, it would have been easier. However God in His wisdom knew His plans for my life and built into me self-discipline that I was able to train my children by example. I was firm in disciplining but loving at the same time. I taught them to be humble and to have respect for other people especially those who are older than them. I wanted them to have a sound and broad education. Although I was not "Born Again" I made sure they attended church service with me on Sundays which they always did enjoy. I remembered then Rev. Payne always gathered children around himself and ministered to them before the adult service. He interacted with them by asking Biblical questions and gave them sweets when they got the answer right. Sometimes when I was too tired to attend a service the children would practically drag me out of bed to go to church. They always wondered why their father would not attend service with us but would go play tennis instead, but thanks be to God, Jesus now reigns in his life and going to church is now a priority on Sundays. Since I met Christ I have stopped being anxious over my children. I now commit everything concerning them to God and I have seen the Mighty Hand of God in their lives, changing a bad situation into a testimony. When they were growing up I always encouraged them to bring their friends home. I must know the friends that they are going out with as well as their parents. I didn't allow them to spend the night at a friend's house. I didn't allow that at all! Once they started going out with a friend, especially the girls, I liked to know the background of that friend. I did encourage them to bring their boyfriends and girlfriends home. Once I don't approve of a relationship especially with my daughters I would tell them once and not say it to them again. Then I would start praying and if it's really what I am thinking, God always intervenes and I see the relationship not continuing. However if one keeps insisting on a 'No' with children especially when it comes to boy/girl relationships, they tend to still want to have it their own way. So I have discovered that prayer works more than what you can do. You can talk until 'you're blue in the face', they may not listen but if all you do after telling them is pray, then you allow the Lord to work on their hearts." She recalled a time she attended one of Billy Graham's meetings as she went on speaking relating the progress concerning bringing up her children. "I remember once that I was so anxious about one of my children that, I was almost at the stage of giving up. At this time I heard that the man of God, Billy

Graham was coming to London. I was here in London at that time; he was ministering outside London. I invited a few people to come along and we went to the crusade. That very day his ministration was, *Don't give up on any child.* He used himself as a testimony as he talked about his sons whom he said, his wife and himself had to stay awake sometime till 2 am in the morning for the boys to come back home. They didn't give up but kept praying and asking God for the Holy Spirit to take control and change them. I thought within myself as he spoke that this was a minister known all over the world because I was getting so anxious within myself that despite all my commitments in God's work at different levels my child was going astray. When I heard his own testimony I was encouraged not to give up. Today his sons are men of God and they are taking over from him, one of them is actually stepping into his shoes. If I had not gone I would not have heard and this is what has helped me to raise my children, hearing other people's experiences. I learn from other people. Actually I don't know what would have happened to my family and I if we had not met Christ. People always tell me, "Aren't you lucky, your children are this, are that", but it is not me, it is God! The psalmist says, "*once I was young and now am old, I have not seen the righteous forsaken or his seed begging bread*" (paraphrased). This is how God has been making a way. Even if they had to leave a school, God will bring another one that was even better than where they were. God has been in control. When we are faithful to Him He takes care of every other thing for us."

I gazed intently at her as I listened. It seemed as if she was giving a sermon. It had depth of thought. It was factual and frank. I appreciated it.

Oluremi Ayida added, "With children you must not relax in committing their every step to God, dedicating and rededicating them to the Almighty God daily because satan is always after them especially the children of godly parents. As you pray over them you will see them coming to Christ one by one. We must know that some things can only be built in our children's lives through prayer. The promise of God is that we and our household should be saved (Acts 16:31). Since my new birth I never stop sharing the Word of God with my children. I never allow any good thing or success or promotion in the family to go without letting them know it is by the grace of God and that the glory should go to Him. When God provides any of them with a new car or house, they come to me to pray and thank God for it and dedicate it to God. The Bible says we should teach our children the way of the Lord..." (Proverbs 22:6)

Oluremi remarked that it is wonderful when your children and grandchildren know you as a praying mother. She stated that her grandchildren request her prayers when they have anything to pray about or sometimes when they are in difficulty, it's also the same with their parents. She added saying as they stayed in the place of prayer together God is so faithful. He takes the glory and He answers the prayer. Recounting a conversation she had with one of her grandchildren, "My grandson, Laolu, who is aged seven had sports in school, he said, "Grandma, its been raining and our sports day is tomorrow. Please pray that there should be no rain tomorrow!" I said, "All right let us pray" as we knelt down together. On that day he came back from school and said "Grandma, it didn't rain!" It's nice when the children know you like this and that they can come and ask questions about JESUS. When you practise what you say and they see it, it's wonderful! Children learn from action more than your talking. As parents, our actions are an influential teaching tool. They will either reinforce or undermine the things you teach your children. We must ask God to help us make our lifestyle worth imitating," said Oluremi Ayida interestingly. She must have prayed with the Elijah kind of anointing for it not to have rained!

As a wife, Oluremi Ayida said her marriage was not without its own challenges. "When I started FBC, we had a study on *Communication in the Home*, I learnt we should pray for our husbands. I started praying. Instead of finding faults with my husband and quarrelling over some of his behaviour that did not go well with me, I started praying to God to change me to be a patient wife and to help him overcome his weaknesses. God answered my prayers! I have discovered that when anything is hurting you, put it to prayer and when you take it to God, He just finds a way of sorting it out for you. This has given me comfort and progress in my marriage. As I read and studied the Bible my behaviour and attitude began to change. I became less self-centred and I saw myself seeking others' interest rather than only my own. I became accommodating and my husband also began to see the change in me too; not nagging, not asking too many questions like, "Why are you late coming home? Why do you not care about how I feel?"

and reading something into what was not there. I always advise young couples, in pre-marriage counselling that for a marriage to be God's way and for the couple to overcome marriage problems, Christ must be the foundation of the marriage. My first task as a marriage counsellor is to lead the couple to accept Christ as their Lord and Saviour if they are not already "Born again". As I have also tasted marriage as an unbeliever and as a believer. As a Christian, Christ becomes your Counsellor and in any problem He helps you to solve it. In times of difficulty God will uphold you to carry the burden until He shows you the way out of it (I Corinthians 10:13). Therefore to have a successful marriage it's there in the Bible; to raise up your children, it's there in the Bible; to have a good relationship with your neighbours, it's there in the Bible; and if you are a true Christian, you would put it into practice. The Word of God is complete; from cradle to grave He's there. He's there for you, if only you will tap into Him. This is what has made a difference in my life! Thank God for not allowing me to waste my life on this Earth because it is a wasted life to live without Christ, and the Word of God. If you don't know the Word that gives light, it's a wasted life! Even if you wait until you're on your death bed and you then give your life to Christ, yes, you would go to heaven but you would have wasted your life here as you would not have fulfilled the purpose of God. Like the thief on the cross, do you know what fulfilment he would have enjoyed in life if he didn't wait until he was on the cross to say "remember me"? He was saved all right! But, he wasted the time that God gave him here on Earth even though he would be in paradise. So this is the essence of it, that our children might not waste their lives but to come to know God. I envy people, the younger generation, who have come to know the Lord at an early age. How I wished I had followed Christ when He touched my life as a youth." Those were golden words and perhaps another sermon, enough to save a soul! Oluremi Ayida spoke passionately of her faith in Christ.

"It's better late than never but thank God for His mercy," I prompted.

Responding excitingly, "Yes! I Thank God for His mercies. Though I was in my fifties when I met Christ in April 1982 at the StoneCroft Bible Study classes, I am so grateful for the hand of salvation He extended to me and the response I made."

She continued speaking in high spirit:

"I've come a long way I must say. God has brought me a long way because my Dad wasn't a practising Christian, my mum an 'Alhaja' (a practising female Muslim that has visited Mecca) and whatever I have been in my Christian walk is by the grace of God. Unlike what God helped me to do for my children by taking them to church, encouraging them, nobody encouraged me in my own time to serve God. Whatever I heard about Christ was from school and it was from there that I started wanting to go to church."

According to Oluremi Ayida her progress is founded on God's grace, basically by Him through others and herself and at the pace He has mapped out for her as an individual.

In one of the top ten life lessons from Noah's ark by Dr James S. Vuocolo it is said that speed is not always an advantage. The cheetahs were on board, but so were the snails and they all arrived safely on dry ground at the very same time according to God's plan and purposes. Our will however plays an important role in walking in and accomplishing God's purpose for our lives as He has given us the freewill to choose and make decisions in line with His word.

Success is a journey, not a destination.
Ben Sweetland

12

HER PROSPERITY

Both riches and honour come from You, and you reign over all.
In Your hand is power and might;
in Your hand it is to
make great and to give strength to all.
1 Chronicles 29: 12

Beloved, I pray that you may prosper
In all things and be in health,
Just as your souls prospers.
3 John 2

Prosperity to so many people has different meanings. Literally it is described as a state of success and good fortune. It is said that to prosper means to get on well, to succeed.

There are quite a number of schools of thought that have made statements all with the intention of defining prosperity.

One school of thought says:

"Prosperity is not in accumulation of wealth or material things. Prosperity is using what God has given you in advancing the kingdom of God."

Another puts it:

"The currency in the world of success is time; your respect for time is a prediction of your financial future."

A school of thought has it that,

"Wealth is the product of man's capacity to think, wisdom being the commander of wealth."

Another states:

"True prosperity is enjoying God's rest; prosperity is not the availability of cash but the availability of light. It is in the attainment of God's goal and purpose."

Another school of thought shares:

"Trading with God's talent in your life guarantees your prosperity and advances your destiny."

Another says:

"Adequate and healthy perception of people is the key to wealth."

Another has it that:

"Money waits for you at the place of your assignment."

Lastly:

"Prosperity literally means 'to help on the road' or 'to reach successfully' – God wants to give us what we need to help us on the road so that we can successfully reach the destiny He has for us. God is not intimidated by the things we have nor does He hold valueless the physical, temporal realm in which we live (See Matthew 6: 25-33) But 'things' aren't the stuff life is made of. There is a realm He calls us to that is 'more real': It is spiritual, it is invisible and it is eternal (See 2 Corinthians 4:18) That is where the real treasure is!"

It is of utmost importance to see what the Bible says concerning this, as it stands not as a school of thought of man's mind but as the mind of God, His Word, that carries finality by the attending life and power of God.

Both riches and honour come from You,
And you reign over all.
In Your hand is power and might;
In Your hand it is to make great
And to give strength to all.

The New Testament reveals

Beloved, I pray that you may prosper
in all things and be in health,
Just as your soul prospers.

It is an established truth that God wants His children to prosper. In telling the story of His handmaiden and her testifying to God's faithfulness in fulfilling His Word over the lives of His people, I asked Oluremi Ayida to describe her life of prosperity. To this she reflects then tells me.

"I think that in every step, God has been leading me and for me to have met my husband and married him, it is God's providence. It was God who arranged it. As I said I wasn't born with a silver spoon in my mouth and neither was my husband but as it is, he is brilliant. He went to Kings College and Oxford University. He came back and got a job with the Federal Government and quickly rose to be the Head of Service and Secretary to the government under different Heads of State. So with this he became well known and respected in the Civil Service. How could it have been? I think I see the work of God in all this preparing me to be where He wants me to be. So that his name is well heard of in Nigeria not for bad, but for good, for integrity, for honesty. God gave him all that!" Oluremi Ayida disclosed that her husband's position and acceptance in the country was part of the way God used to prepare the ground for the ministry work for her.

She recalled the day when a lady judge visited the Ayida's house for the very first time. Oluremi Ayida said that the lady expressed much surprise at what she saw as she gave compliments to her and the beautiful house. She spoke of Mrs Ayida's much involvement in God's work despite all that she had. According to Oluremi, she said, "The visit left the lady with something to think about."

According to her, there is always a large turn-out of people attending evangelistic outreaches held at her house under the FBC ministry. She states: "So this is what God has done, He has prospered the family to use us as an outlet to draw people to Himself. When I retired my pension wasn't very much, but I have lacked nothing. At that time I wanted something to do, so I went into textiles. Together with a friend of mine, we got contracts for office interior decorations. Shortly after, I joined the FBC and with this I had no more time to seek gainful employment because of my commitment to the work of God. God was using my husband to meet my needs so that I was able to go on with the work. When we started FBC it was not easy getting the study books to Nigeria. I advanced the money for ordering the books and members reimbursed me. The books were usually shipped to London; I would then bring them to Lagos. I was able to do this because my children were schooling in England and I had to be with them during the half terms and end of year holidays. With this arrangement in place we were never short of study books. As the group multiplied and more books were needed,

I could not afford the funding involved at this time and the books became too heavy to bring as my personal luggage to Nigeria. This was the time when we wrote to StoneCroft applying for permission to print the books in Nigeria." As though to confirm what she had been saying she paused and turned herself slightly backwards and continued speaking, "You can see..." pointing to the veranda outside the sitting room's sliding glass doors. "Outside there are four big cartons. They are Selwyn Hughes's autobiography. We've sold off what we took to Nigeria initially so I am taking back more. I have a hundred copies to take back with me. The CWR has given us permission to print it but it will still take a while before the approval comes through so I will still have to carry the books this way." She added in a lighter tone of humour, "If I was doing my own business to keep body and soul together, I wouldn't have been able to do this. Rather I'd be carrying only what I would be selling. The books are more than my baggage allowance but my husband and other family members who happen to be around at the time would take some also. So this is how I've been taking the books back especially when they are urgently needed."

To Oluremi Ayida God's provisions for her, has enabled her to be a voluntary worker in the ministry. "So this is how God has met my provision and how He has prospered me. He brought that prosperity using my husband at all times. Before I can say, 'God I need this, Father show me who to go to,' He will lead me in my heart whom to go to. As I go to the person and tell of my request the response is always positive because God has already prepared them." Whenever the ministry is involved in any project that demands a lot of financial commitment such as the visit of Rev. Selwyn Hughes or other Evangelistic programmes which the ministry's fund cannot accommodate, Mrs Ayida has learnt to depend on the Lord for direction to receiving provisions.

She recalled various situations she had needed to be led of God for His provisions. "Whenever Selwyn Hughes is coming we raise money to do quite a number of things. Publicity is a major aspect and it is very expensive. At this time I go to the National Television Authority (NTA) and Channels Television and God is so gracious to us that they air our adverts free of charge as part of their free informative programmes to the Nigerian public. That is God prospering the work using others to prosper it." She added swiftly and brightly as if putting an addendum to her earlier statement, "Channels Television has been one of FBFM's partners in promoting the Gospel, and the wife of the Managing Director is one of our members."

With a tone of joy and enthusiasm Oluremi narrates further: "When I said we wanted to build the Headquarters we sent circulars out for people to contribute. They contributed freely, willingly! Then I said we needed a lift, as we couldn't be going up and down the staircase all the time. Willingly they gave! This is God prospering the work because if they didn't give, the work won't go on." There was a time the ministry had to raise a large amount of money to cover for the time lapse in sending the 'Cover to Cover' books to Nigeria. Some copies of the books had been sent to Nigeria for sale to meet the January reading time but they did not arrive in Nigeria until August. The Publishers incurred a lot of costs due to the delay. A number of members were called on for aid, which they responded to thus resolving the issue as Mrs Ayida recalled the initial take off of the 'Cover to Cover' books being published.

God's provisions are necessary in doing His will. When God speaks, He speaks for a purpose, and for every purpose of God, there is a divine provision that attends to its accomplishment. The ministry of the Word and prayer which Oluremi Ayida has committed her life to, according to God's grace and ability upon her life has touched many lives for Christ not only in Nigeria but abroad. The thirst and zeal of seeing people gathering together in fellowship under the umbrella of Jesus Christ, the Redeemer of mankind, remains unquenchable in her. Desiring to see lives being transformed she makes the best use of divine opportunities that comes her way. Speaking Mrs Ayida recalls, "I remember some time ago inviting our daddy in the Lord, Pastor Adeboye for a luncheon at my house here in London. As we drove down to the house he turned to me and said humorously in Yoruba language, "Ko si enito nwale e lofe" (meaning, "it's going to cost me paying you this visit!") my answer was "yes!" laughing as she spoke. "I had already invited some ladies to the house for lunch where the servant of God would preach and do his favourite thing – winning souls for his Heavenly Father." Bursting into more laughter she said, "Daddy Adeboye said, 'I'm going to pay for this!' and I still affirmed telling him, 'yes, you are!'" as we both had a long laugh over it. She remarked gracefully, "I give glory to God for this great General of God that has come my way and has given so much of himself to nurture FBC ministry to achieve its mission. I can say with boldness that fifty percent of FBC's spiritual growth is ascribed to the men of God who have nurtured us especially Pastor Adeboye who started with us when we had a membership of six ladies. May the good Lord continue to bless and prosper these men of God that He has used and is still using to bless FBFM."

Believe in the Lord your God, so shall ye be established; believe His prophets, so shall you prosper.

2 Chronicles 20:20

In a low tone as if depicting a deep sense of appreciation acknowledging God's provisions to her, Oluremi Ayida whispered "It's God! It's God! He's our source and will continue to be in Jesus Name. I have come to the conclusion that all He has given us is to use to His glory. It is a crime for anyone not to acknowledge God as the provider of all good things we own and to use it for His glory. The Bible says that all good things come from Him (James 1:17) We must not think that it is by our power or by our might." Mrs Ayida shared the truth that the state of being successful comes by the empowerment of God.

But you shall remember the LORD thy God: for it is He that gives power to get wealth, that He may establish His covenant which He swore to your fathers, as it is this day.

Deuteronomy 8:18

Oluremi Ayida affirmed, "Everything He has given me is for the promotion of His Kingdom. Our children too. God has given us children and if we give them back to Him He will use them for His glory. I told God that I wanted Him to use my daughter who's an Obstetrician and a Gynaecologist for His glory. Today I meet many people telling me how God has used her to help them. That is God! When you give the children to Him He will use them to His praise and you will see them being a channel of help, God blessing and using them to be a blessing to people. That is what I call true prosperity. Prosperity that is used to the benefit of humanity and to the glory of God."

Her two daughters, Alero and Gbubemi and her three sons, Omatseyin, Abidemi and Amaju are all doing well in their fields of endeavour and stand as God's prosperity and His wonderful blessing to the Allison and Oluremi Ayida family for which they are very grateful to God.

Suffice it to say that the provisions of God encompasses every aspect of our lives: spiritual, the physical and emotional and the material.

Oluremi Ayida testifies to the good health she has enjoyed in God over the many years back. Her recalling to memory of the time when she was very sick, being carried by her husband on his back as they waded through the flood to get to the hospital where she got medical treatment for her acute appendicitis continues to make her thankful to God. She spoke intently, "God spared my life and if He spared my life and I refused Him I would have wasted what He has saved me for. Oluremi Ayida disclosing the present arthritic condition of her legs added with humour, "I suppose that if I didn't have that, I'll still be jumping all over thinking I'm fifty because I feel young inside. God has a way of slowing us down one way or the other." Like the Apostle Paul whom the Lord made His grace sufficient for the 'thorn in his flesh', Mrs Ayida agrees. "Yes, yes, His grace is sufficient. I have been praying, I said I wanted to have a knee replacement operation for many years now, but I have not had any release to go ahead yet. So for the moment His grace is sufficient and will always be.

Appreciating God not only for the prosperity of her health but also that of her husband Oluremi Ayida says, "For my husband He has prospered his health, I must say I thank God. He has had two strokes and by God's grace he is alive today, healthy going around, agile. To God be the glory great things he has done for us."

The love of God is facilitated by giving as Paul writes in the eighth verse of the eighth chapter of his second book to the Corinthian church. Giving is the only biblical way to prove the sincerity of one's love and to be rich towards God. Oluremi delights in sharing her prosperity with others.

"I love giving out of the substance God gives me, I want to be a blessing to other lives," Mrs Ayida tells.

In her characteristic giving attitude Oluremi Ayida has being used by God to be a blessing to so many lives in different forms, personally and through the ministry. Many women have received financial help from the ministry and numerous others have been set up in businesses. Many have been helped to have gainful education that would enable them to stand right in the future and be a pride to the Nation. Eight hundred inmates of Majidun, a home for destitutes in Ikorodu in Lagos State are fed twice weekly by the FBFM. Through her sponsorship two catholic priests received their training when they had requested for sponsors to train priests. Her giving attitude attested to by many continues to stand as a reflection of her covenant of prosperity.

A generous man devices
generous things and by
generosity he shall stand.
Isaiah 32:8 (NKJV)

Divine prosperity is not a momentary, passing phenomenon, but rather it is an ongoing, progressing, state of success and well-being of the total man: spirit, soul and body. God does not want us to unduly emphasise on any one area. We must maintain a balance.

We shall be judged according to our privileges, according to the light we have received, and the obedience we have rendered to it, not only outwardly, but inwardly, according to our rebellion or submission to God; according to our loyalty and obedience to Him; in our hearts as well as in our lives.

Catherine Booth

Oluremi with Mrs Bunmi
Adeniji Pioneer FBC Nigeria

Below: Oluremi
with Lucille Sollenberger,
FBC Bible Study writer

FBFM Board with
Father-in-the-Lord
Pastor E.A. Adeboye,
2001

Ministry A

*Pastor Adeboye
& Oluremi
Ayida, 2006*

*Selwyn Hughes' first
visit with David Rivett
and FBC member
Cecilia Ibru in 1991*

*Oluremi Ayida
with Selwyn Hughes*

Ministry B

A cross section of guests at a Marriage Seminar, Unilag, 1991

Left: 2nd Visit – Ministers Seminar National Theatre 1993

Below:

3rd Visit –– Ministers Seminar National Theatre 1998

Ministry C

Dedication of FBFM Secretariat, 2001

From left: Mrs Toyin Adedoyin, Pastor Adeboye, Mrs Oluremi Ayida and Mrs Cecilia Ibru at the official opening of the Headquarters, 2001

Selwyn Hughes blessing FBFM Headquarters, 2001

Ministry D

Selwyn Hughes & Jeanette Barwick visit to the FBFM Headquarters, 2001

Above: With Pastor (Mrs) Folu Adeboye at the Bible College Graduation 1993

Right: With some FBC members visit to Garden of Gethsemene, 1993

*At an Art &
Craft class
Children's camp*

*Marriage
Seminar,
Abuja
Nigeria,
2001*

*A Ministers'
Seminar in
Lagos*

Ministry F

At StoneCroft Ministries Conference in Kansas City, 2004

Remi

At Selwyn Hughes Autobiography presentation in England, 2004

Ministry G

Award presentation to Oluremi Ayida at
Women's CAN Lagos Branch, 2006

Ministry H

13

HER PERSECUTIONS AND PAIN

Why are you cast down, O my soul?
And why are you disquieted within me?
Hope in God: For I shall yet praise Him ...
Psalm 43: 5

But the God of all grace,
who hath called us unto His eternal glory by Christ Jesus,
after that you have suffered a while,
make you perfect, stablish, strengthen, settle you.
1 Peter 5:10

Tests, trials and temptations are commonplace in the journey of life. As the people of God we learn how to put our trust in Him because only by Him can we be victorious over life's storms and challenges. Times as this are meant to make us completely focused on God and on His infinite ability to deliver by His Word and His Spirit. The Bible reveals various people who at one time or the other in their lives faced tests, trials, temptations and recorded defeats or victories as the case may be. Such times brought out a picture of their humanity, their attitudes, their trust in God and the divinity of God.

Every detail of our life is embedded in God even though there is always the role of God and the role of man unto victory and accomplishment. However it is noteworthy to state that whether our trust be high or at the lowest ebb, regardless of where we are with our faith, God remains the only One that is mighty to save and deliver beyond what our finite minds can even comprehend!

"Not by might nor by power, but by my Spirit,"
says the LORD of Hosts.
Zechariah 4:6

Oluremi Ayida reveals her share of these times as she recalled events and happenings in her life and ministry over the many years.

Dating back to her career days, Oluremi Ayida as a Public Health Nurse was seconded by the Lagos City Council to start one of the Community Health Centres. It was to be the one on the mainland at Randle Avenue in Surulere. Under her professional direction and discretion the Surulere Health Centre was set up, equipped and staffed with her being the administrative head of the place. For about two years the centre was running very well until she went overseas for a Public Health administrative course to enhance the work. She came back and still continued with her duties until a critical moment emerged. She suddenly received a letter directing her back to the Lagos City Council, stating that she was not of Lagos origin and that another lady was to be posted to the position she occupied. It was met with a series of petitions from her to the authorities. She referred them to records that showed she had a 'right' in Lagos State. Her mother was from Isale-Eko she says (that is, from the interiors of the Lagos Island), from the family of the Dosunmus'.

"It was a tug of war. The Doctor in charge was really after me and I wrote petitions but by the grace of God He won the battle for me. It was a tough battle but God took control and I remained at the post for another ten years until I retired so they were unable to move me away from that office. So that was how God helped me even though I didn't 'know' Him. He helped me," she said.

After her retirement, in 1976 she joined the Friendship Bible Coffees fellowship in 1982 and in a short while became very much occupied in the work. Another critical period was approaching. An 'invasion' had started; her home was being affected. The 'man of the house' felt it was getting too much, he was not happy about it, it had reached a crescendo and a family meeting had to be urgently put in place to sort out the pressing matter. One could possibly say that the pressing matter was a 'divine encroachment'. She could not handle the issue. As much as she tried, she still found herself falling short of the mutual agreement arrived at during the family meeting to reduce or if possible, stop her newly found commitment to God and fellowship activities. In her inadequacy and failings she turned the matter to God saying, "God how can I serve you? I cannot give the best of my time to what You are calling me to do, so You have to help me, You have to …"

This heart cry brought God on the spot. His ability and adequacy took over. The divine inroad to the family was not meant to disintegrate it in anyway or to subvert headship authority but to consolidate it in His everlasting will and purpose, a divine privilege and honour!

But I want you to know that the head of every man is Christ,
the head of woman is man,
and the head of Christ is God.
1 Corinthians 11:3

Thus He began to release and channel His grace as Oluremi puts it, "Then gradually from total opposition they started tolerating, then from tolerating they started accepting and from accepting they started getting involved themselves! That is how God works, grace coming gradually." Just as the situation in the home was being gradually brought under God's control, Oluremi still had that of her friends to sort out! Speaking, "I had no more interest in going to parties, my social activities were reducing and I was becoming unpopular. My interest had shifted to Bible study, prayer meetings and fellowship groups. I wanted to hear more about Christ."

The zeal of her new life in Christ made Oluremi Ayida much more involved in church work at the local level. She did more of Bible reading and expositions in the church. She got involved in helping to organise activities or in some cases in charge of organising and co-ordinating activities for the church. Her new life in Christ and her zeal for His work was not without its own challenges amidst associates.

This brings to mind the life of Peter, the chief disciple of Jesus. He was a 'reed' turned into a 'rock' by the prophetic declaration of the Master upon his life. He received a complete change of his nature, status, and identity and in fact his entire life. This began to manifest through him after the baptism of the Holy Ghost on the day of Pentecost. The same Peter who shuddered from men and denied Jesus became the one who stood boldly before a multitude in the face of challenge and contention and gave a sermon that about three thousand souls were saved. Something definitely had to have taken place in the life of Peter. It was no longer Peter the reed; a divine transformation had taken place by the Spirit of God. He was no longer walking in the superficial understanding of who Christ is but a supernatural understanding by the Holy Ghost!

Like Peter, Oluremi Ayida's faith in Christ had become that of a personal conviction, a living reality and relationship with the Lord, a lone walk that she had opposition to put up with. Mrs Ayida recalled that it took the Godly wisdom of the Vicar to give his approval of the introduction and set up of the Marriage Counselling Ministry in the local Church which was initiated by her but was initially opposed. Still given the opportunity to go on with what she believed will be beneficial to the church at large, the Counselling ministry took off and it has since been in operation for many years.

Her understanding of the Bible changed. It had received illumination by the Holy Spirit; the Word of God had changed from being 'letter' to 'Spirit and Life.' Sometimes when she is opportuned to discuss the scriptures with other people it could get quite lively in some cases, as there could be differences in interpretation and understanding.

It is the Spirit who gives life; the flesh profits nothing.
The words that I speak to you are spirit, and they are life.
John 6:63

According to Oluremi Ayida, the work of the ministry is not without its own challenges, it had teething problems that brought about internal differences. Initially the idea of introducing *Every Day with Jesus* with the Friendship Bible Coffees fellowship was opposed. It was thought by some to be an infringement and digression on the policies of the parent body. This disagreement eventually got to the knowledge of the leadership in America. This period for her was a time of opposition and persecution. She was almost giving up on the work as the devil always whispered tauntingly to her mind not to continue with the work where she was not being appreciated or remunerated. Her appointment as the leader was also opposed by some, while the majority gave their approval and supported her leadership. This situation consequently delayed the approval of the printing of the FBC study books in Nigeria from the StoneCroft ministries even though it had been requested for from Nigeria since 1984.

However by God's divine intervention issues began to be sorted out. The fiftieth year anniversary celebration of the StoneCroft International Ministries in August 1988 was one of the platforms that the Lord used to give approval to the ministry in Nigeria. Attended by about twelve members from Nigeria, who gave an

124

impressive performance Mrs Ayida says, "God opened the door by that celebration. The leadership were convinced of the good work which God was doing in Nigeria through us and it was at this occasion that we were given the approval to print the study books. So that's satan wanting to put a break in the work of God. I thank God that despite the persecutions and hardships God allowed it for sometime, but today He's perfecting His purpose. Persecution and hardships has made me look at myself and see where I am failing and to make amends. Every persecution has been a promotion for the ministry and me. I thank God for the fruit of the Holy Spirit – patience, which these experiences and more have produced in my life. Though it has not been easy to produce it in me because impatience has been the sin that easily besets me but thanks be to God, the Holy Spirit who is working in me daily to make me be like Christ and because of patience I do not react to negative things said about me," she said.

"Praying for my children has drawn me closer to God and has brought me to my knees, crying to Him on their behalf. I knew the grace of God because of the boys. If I hadn't had difficulty with them and everything had gone smoothly with them as with the girls, I probably would have thought that it was my cleverness and my goodness or by my power, but that 'thorn in the flesh' brought me closer to God. It made me look to Him, focus on Him and I thank God that when I sit back now looking at the past, I would not exchange it for anything. I thank Him for it. See what has come out of it – a great ministry!

From her walk with the Lord over the years, Oluremi Ayida revealed that Christians sometimes do not know when they are falling short, when there is a relaxing in fellowship with God but as she puts it, "There's always an alarm clock, a check."

"If I get distracted from God, He always sounds His alarm. Things start to go wrong and I am not at peace. Immediately I go on my knees and start spending time with the Lord. I think He does that to us all unless we choose not to listen or be sensitive to Him. It's like one has a rope on the neck of a dog and if the dog is going astray you pull the rope and when the rope is taut, the dog comes back. God has a way of doing that to His children. Christians must always be sensitive to God's alarm. Your alarm may be different from mine but He helps you to know warning signs."

Being the human beings that we are and not in anyway trying to deny the existence of unpleasant situations in life, I humbly asked Oluremi about her attitude, her tenacity to hold on in the face of adversity. To this she responded:

"My first reaction to unpleasant situations before I became a Christian was to fight for my rights and stand my ground, using all the power I could muster to change the situation, which would sometimes end in disaster. Now that Christ is in my life my immediate reaction is to be still and I say a little prayer in my heart calling on the Holy Spirit, my best Friend, to take control. Immediately I get direction on what I should do. I find myself doing things that would correct the situation and put it back on the right course. Sometimes it is easy and at times it is difficult especially when God wants to use the situation to teach me a lesson and promote me through it. If I have a misunderstanding with anyone whether I am wronged or I am the one in the wrong, I never approach the situation without first praying. The heart of a man is in the hand of the Almighty God and He is the only One who can control the heart of a man. My God always steps in and resolves the problem. It may be immediately but sometimes it takes months or even years, but He never fails. What I have discovered in resolving problems is to keep away from anger. The approach! That is what God has given me now. One cannot be angry and be calm at the same time. So a Christian's reaction to any problem, is to turn one's mind to God. Ask Him for His help in the situation. As a Christian worshipping 'God in spirit and in truth,' He uses unpleasant situations to make us grow, to promote us and to use us to help others who will be facing that same kind of trial as one would have a testimony to encourage that person. He won't give us more than what we can bear (1 Corinthians 10:13), because as Pastor Adeboye says *"there is no promotion without passing an examination,"* Oluremi Ayida said, laughing as she spoke sharing from her wealth of experience. She testifies of eventually becoming friends with those who have really hurt her, fellowshipping with them. Some come to her asking her to pray with them. "God has granted me the grace that they are now my friends, we are now children of the Most High because the Love of Christ is in us. They learn from the ministry and from me."

Rick Warren in his book *Purpose Driven Life* says: "*Problems force you to focus on God, draw you closer to others in fellowship,*

126

build Christ-like character, provides you with a ministry, and gives you a testimony."

Consider it pure joy, my brothers,
whenever you face trial of many kinds,
because you know that the testing of your faith
develops perseverance.
Perseverance must finish its work so that you may be mature
and complete, not lacking anything.
James 1: 2-3

I am not afraid of storms for I am learning to sail my ship.
Lousia May Alcott

14

HER PROSPECTS

But those who wait on the Lord shall renew
Their strength; they shall mount up with wings
As eagles, they shall run and not be weary,
They shall walk and faint.
Isaiah 40: 31

Brethren, I do not count myself to have apprehended;
But one thing I do,
Forgetting those things which are behind
And reaching forward to those things which are ahead.
I press toward the goal for the prize
of the upward call of God in Christ Jesus.
Philippians 3: 13, 14

Here comes the future. Insight, foresight, expectations, aspirations and desires; the vision and strides that constitute the features of the future.

With all sense of modesty, Oluremi Ayida has no doubt come a long way by the grace and mercy of the living God in life and ministry. Being sustained by the breath of the Almighty and being changed from glory to glory by the Spirit of the Lord unto the accomplishment of God's purposes to the fullness on earth.

The great Psalmist declared that for *as long as he lived, the earth shall be filled with the glory of the Lord!* and he had the testimony *that after he had served his own generation by the will of God, he joined his fathers* (Acts 13:36).

I asked Oluremi Ayida to let us in as much as it is given to her into her aspirations and expectations of the future. For the ministry she began.

"What I envisage for the future of the ministry to be is an organisation that not only caters for one group of people but catering for children, singles, families and the elderly. Catering for them not just physically but mostly spiritually. Even when I talk of the aged or elderly, it is about encouraging them to walk closer to God, to be sure they have eternal life and make them to be sure of where they are going to spend eternity. It is also to bring them together to fellowship with one another so as to prevent loneliness which is the bane of old age."

Using herself as an example. "What will I have been doing now if I didn't have a relationship with God?" she asked.

The aim of this as Oluremi Ayida puts it, is for the elderly being armed with the knowledge of God and His word, would enable them to help the younger ones by interpreting what they have experienced and relating it spiritually to them. This places on them the responsibility of being Mentors to the younger ones. Apart from getting the old people to read the Bible, Oluremi Ayida spoke of the ministry's plan to have a 'Home' for them. She described it as a temporary accommodation and stopover place to house the elderly in a comfortable and conducive environment whilst their families are away and when there is no one to look after them, a place where they can be with others for that period.

For what the ministry has planned for the children, Oluremi recalled her days in school when they had morning assembly. She says, "We started the day with the Word of God and we sang a hymn before going to classes. But nowadays they don't do that any more since the government took possessions of the schools but thank God, some states, for example Lagos State, have returned the schools to the missions." Continuing she revealed, "This is why we want to reach the children for the Lord. We want a ministry that can reach out to them with what they are not getting from the schools. This desire made us to start importing *Every Day with Jesus* for children that is, YP's and TOPZ for different age groups so that they can read the Word of God which has been printed in cartoon form to suit them. I want us to be able to take it to schools, and make it available to students at a reduced cost. I believe that the children will love it. As they are diligent in reading the Lord will minister to them. We want to reach them at that young age, not just in schools but also in Church Sunday schools and youth clubs.

Still in a tenacious tone Mrs Ayida described the vision for the singles' ministry.

"I want us to be able to run seminars that will interest singles. We will have topics for them such as "How to be a secure woman",

"Understanding yourself and understanding others", "Marriage - God's way" and many more that will enlighten their understanding of God's path for them. Because the only Person who can make them totally whole is Christ, (Spiritual, physical, mental, emotional and marital wholeness). So using the form of seminars to do that will interest the younger ones, the married ones, and build them up. That is an expectation of mine that the ministry will really go more into."

Asking Oluremi how they intend to do that and the things being put into place for implementation, she disclosed that they are commencing the training of people for the work in 2006. They are expecting a team of trainers for the trainees from the CWR in United Kingdom. She added that three members of FBC were sponsored to attend counselling courses in August and November 2005 at CWR. This will enhance the growth of the counselling ministry of FBFM.

She also stated that a three-acre land has been given to the ministry at Lekki Epe Road on the outskirts of the Lagos Island, with plans being in place as to how best to use the land.

Making her vision known she says, "We want to have an FBC Children and Youth Ministry, an Old Peoples' Ministry, a Women's Ministry, something like a village plan. I want a city for FBFM. The Children's holiday camp will be in that city, a resort for members who want to go for a spiritual break. It's a vast land that we've been given. All we want to do now is to start buying more land to add to it. That is my vision." As Oluremi spoke in high spirit with enthusiasm for the future of the ministry, she promptly added as if quickly remembering it, "And then I want us to have an FBFM printing press, an independent printing press. Our vision for FBFM is to cater for the total man: spirit, soul and body."

And the Lord answered me and said:
"Write the vision and make it plain upon tables that he may run that reads it.
For the vision is yet for an appointed time, but at the end it shall speak and not lie though it tarry,
wait for it; because it will surely come, it will not tarry."
Habakkuk 2: 2, 3

Referring to Pastor Austen Ukachi's remark in bringing to light the great prospects awaiting the ministry during the Award Service for

Oluremi Ayida, he said, "Thank God for the strides made so far. The challenge you have before you is far more than you have achieved. What is 140,000 compared to seventy million Christians? The task ahead is much more, work harder, make more connections, ask God to open more doors for the entrance of God's Word. Nothing can transform a man more than the Bible. My earnest prayer is that God will use you to encourage more people to read the Bible."

To this Oluremi Ayida spoke on how the ministry intends to achieve a wider range of cover of readers of EDWJ and other publications in the Nigerian population.

She reflects speaking that one thing she has observed, is how God has been leading the ministry from inception. It has been from a small environment to a big one, from a big place to a bigger one, and from a bigger place to an even bigger one. One step at a time she affirmed. Speaking she puts it: "So we see now that if we are to print five hundred thousand copies every month, we do not have enough facilities for that capacity yet, but He has given us the vision so we can focus on it and He has given us the land already. So even if it is the warehouse we will build first in the city, along side the office complex, we'll do that."

For the Children's Holiday camp, Oluremi Ayida mentioned that at the moment there is no permanent location for the programme. They have often hired the use of a school for the Holiday Camp which has also given the awareness for other people to start such a programme and as a result availability of accommodation becomes inadequate. At the moment the ministry has to make use of the estate of members.

I remarked, "God takes you a step at a time, He sees how faithful you are and then makes provision for the next level, not what one can do by might or by power."

Affirming, Oluremi Ayida responded, "Yes, exactly! We have a story. He gives the space and then fills the space. After filling the space, we have another one. This is how it has been from what I've seen over the years. It's not the volume of work that comes first. He first provides what we need and then tell us what to do with it."

Speaking on her own personal prospects, Oluremi Ayida disclosed, "My personal prospect is that every minute of the day I want to be thinking of God, for Him to always be on my mind. You know you can sit down and be conversing with Him and be talking to Him all the time, I'm able to do this better here in London. It is also my desire to have more time to read the Bible now that the Almighty God, the Jehovah Rapha has restored my sight through surgery I have no more excuse. Do you know I hear more from God when I'm here... every plan, every inspiration and revelation has been mostly from here, as it is often a time of stillness, no activities, no visits unless it is by appointment."

"That is being alone with God," I added.

"I don't do as much now as I did before. When I used to visit, I would go window-shopping, go visiting with people, go to the theatre and the cinema, but now I do that only occasionally. I say "Father, thank you". I have other things to occupy me as well now. I've got the Bible on tape and I sit here for hours listening to it. I am on the book of second Chronicles now and it gives me much joy. When my grandchildren are around me I have more time to play with them, praying with and for them and also for the ministry as I wait on the Lord. Here I can say that I have more time to wait on the Lord, as I don't have to run around as much and get tired. It's when I withdraw from the crowd and I'm alone that I hear from Him. Even my people back home says, 'when Mummy comes back, she is coming back with a new revelation!'" she added amusingly. "So in essence my prospect is to continue to grow in the knowledge and love of God. I want to reach the stage that every thought of my mind is on God and what I can do to glorify Him. I desire to be a woman after God's heart that when He looks down I hope He will be pleased with me. I want to be the delight of His heart. I also want to be like Barnabas (Acts 4:36) encouraging people to follow the way of our Lord and Saviour Jesus Christ and wanting to live a life pleasing to Him. I want by His grace, for God to continue to use me as a channel of His blessing in the Body of Christ. I desire also to hear clearly from Him and that everything I do will be to His glory."

In the course of reading the first book of Chronicles, Mrs Ayida said the Lord just ministered to her as she saw King David appointing singers. Before then she had been feeling guilty because she had always gotten people to come and pray, to hold vigils for the ministry. As she puts it: "I thought I was doing something that was wrong, that I was being lazy. But after reading Chronicles and seeing David appointing people to praise, and to stand in different

132

offices in service to God, I was convinced that I was in line with the Word of God. The new inspiration I have now is a time of praise to Him, so I'm taking this back with me. The Lord ministered to me to inculcate 'Praise time', where we take one day in a month as a group of people to do nothing else but just praise Him for at least one hour. So this is how I get inspiration from God," as she speaks in a joyful tone.

"That's the latest from the Holy Ghost, your best friend!" I humorously remarked, recalling how she refers to Him. Spontaneously with a loud voice she responded, "My best friend Oh! ah, my very best friend!"

Asking Oluremi Ayida of prospects she had for her family, un-hesitantly she spoke. "I want to see my children serving the Lord, worshipping and having a relationship with Him. My prayer is "God if you prolong my life, I want to see one of my children behind the pulpit preaching." I want to see them serving the Lord, working for Him. I want to see them all as workers in the house of God. For this I regularly cry to God in prayers and I am confident that the Lord will grant me my heart's desires."

I like the dreams of the future better than the past.
Thomas Jefferson

15

HER PRAISE

I will sing to the LORD as long as I live:
I will sing praise to my God
while I have my being.
Psalm 104: 33
Come and hear, all who fear God,
And I will declare what He has done
for my soul.
Psalm 66: 16

Recorded in the Bible are words and acts of praise and thanksgiving to God by various people. In different circumstances and situations at different times of their lives, these people testified to God's mighty power attending to them. The adequacy and strength of God being revealed over man's inadequacies and limitations.

He delights in the praise and thanksgiving of His people for who He is and for what He does. A careful look at the entire one hundred and third chapter of the Psalms highlights the features of praise and thanksgiving to God.

For the handmaiden of God, Oluremi Ayida testifies that certain situations in life, which one has gone through, are seen to be giving one joy later on in life. As she asked for the opportunity to put down some of her testimonies saying, "When one now see what one has had doubts and fears over in times past now as a pinnacle of testimony of all that has happened to one, you just thank God! You just want to burst out praising Him continuously that He alone could have done this!"

Sharing the testimonies of her life and ministry for which she is full of praise and thanksgiving to God, Oluremi Ayida began:

"There is no one who hasn't got a problem. I used to envy people who say their children have never given them any problems but I don't any more because it is my children who have brought me to where I am. So I praise Him and I thank God for the children, for the boys especially for the way God has used them to humble me. I call it 'a humbling experience'; as it humbled me before God and made me to be aware that He exists. All I thought I had was nothing but just God's grace. With the girls, I was always eager to go to their schools because I wanted to hear nice things and I got good reports of how well they were doing in their studies. Though my boys also were disciplined, respectful and obedient they preferred playing to studying so it wasn't always a good report and I often went back home sad. I never gave up on them. I spent time with them, encouraging them in the right way through sleepless nights, helping them out with their homework. I organised extra tuition for them. With prayer and supplication and a strong faith in God I was given the victory over satan. Today I can lift up my head and say, 'Father, You have done wonderfully well for me'."

"The lesson I've learnt from that, is that one should not give up on any child and that we should take our problem to God, as I saw that money could not deliver but God alone. They got into good secondary schools and universities. They graduated from university, God did that. So we should never give up and we should bathe our children in prayer. Pray for them regularly for God's purpose to prevail in their lives, and for their lives to glorify God. We must never forget to dedicate them to the Lord, dedicate them regularly in case satan has forgotten that they don't belong to him. As you give to the Lord, He is able to take care of them but if you say that 'they are mine', and you think that they are yours, how are you able to take care of them? Well, satan can do whatever he wants with them and succeed. But when you give them to the Lord He is able to do infinitely much more than you and I could ever think. This is the assurance that I have. I dedicate my home and all that I have to God. There is nothing good that we have that is not from God, nothing. So every good and perfect gift is from God, (James 1:17), why not give Him what is His because He will not struggle with you unless you give it to Him. So the sooner we hand everything to Him, the better for us. That is what I have learnt in my walk with God. Whatever problem I may be having, I have the confidence that God is in control and I know that everything will come together in the end and that it will be a testimony glorifying God. His word that He makes all things work together for good, is one of my favourite verses in the Bible. (Romans 8:28). Today the boys are doing well! God is still working in them. One thing I've discovered now is that I am able to comfort any mother who is going through that difficulty. I could testify that I see so many people coming to me today saying 'Mummy, I want to come and see you.' If it is a marriage problem I've gone through it, if it's over children, I've gone through it, if it is a relationship problem with friends, I've been there. It is also the same with the ministry. That is my first testimony," Oluremi Ayida went on speaking with strength in her voice.

"My second testimony is concerning the children as well. In 1979, the children were all here, and I had come to spend the mid-term holiday with them. There was a little Anglican Church that I usually attended on Sundays with the children. I didn't always pray with them but it was the notion of just going to church. On this beautiful Sunday morning I woke them up to go to church. Daddy wasn't around, he was in Nigeria then. Whilst I made breakfast downstairs I thought the children were getting ready not knowing that they were still sleeping in their rooms upstairs. When I got through I informed the eldest to get the others up, have their breakfast and join me in the church which was just a short walk from the house. Halfway through the service, I had a witness in my heart to go back home. I quickly looked around to see if the children were there, but they were not. Immediately I left for home. As I made my entrance to the house the whole ground floor was filled with smoke, the frying pan on the cooker was on fire, as I had forgotten to turn off the cooker in my haste to leave, whilst all my five children were still sleeping upstairs. The house was such that as one comes in, the kitchen is on the left and the sitting room adjacent it. A few steps along takes one to the staircase. There was no way that one could possibly come down if there had been a fire on the ground floor. I quickly turned off the cooker and looked for something, a rag to beat the fire off and opened the windows. I then ran upstairs calling the children and brought them all out. Who did that for me? God rescued my children sparing their lives and removing misery from my life, as I've heard of children being burnt in houses. At this time I didn't know God but He removed calamity from my life and filled my mouth with songs of praise. So this is a testimony that prepared me. God sparing and giving me this joy is for a reason. He did not allow it to be said of me that I have had such a miserable life and that this is what brought me to Him. No! That will not be my testimony for knowing God. I thank God for that!"

Giving her third testimony, Oluremi Ayida recalled. "I was praying one day. This was in Lagos and the Holy Spirit said, "Fast for seven days." This was some years ago. So I called my sister. My mind was thinking about tragedy in the ministry. So my sister, Mrs Nanna and I fasted and prayed and we completed the seven days. We prayed at random as the Holy Spirit led us, for God to protect the ministry and the members' lives. We then touched on our families, our children who are in different places and ourselves. Then on the eighth day I had left the office and was on my way home. As I arrived home, my husband who would usually have still been in the office said he had been trying to reach me on the phone but could not get me. He said our daughter, Gbubemi, had had an accident in London. He said it was a ghastly accident and that she was in hospital but was all right. I asked, "But what happened?" At this time she was working in Ealing General Hospital as a Senior Registrar, and she drove every day to work. As she was driving that day, there was a traffic hold up and she joined the queue. Suddenly a petrol tanker coming in the opposite direction lost control and ran into four or five cars. My daughter's car was the last one in the queue. The tanker landed on her bonnet. Initially they couldn't get her out of the car; it was a Mercedes Benz. After some effort from the rescue team she was brought out covered with a blanket and put in a waiting ambulance. The car was a total write-off. When she spoke to me, she said, 'Mummy, when the tanker was on top of me, I thought I had died.' She said she wasn't fully conscious but she could still see people moving around." With a high tone of voice and with her hands in motion, narrating, Oluremi continued. "Do you know? She didn't even get a single scratch, nobody could believe it! When the photograph of the collision was brought out, one would have thought nobody could come out of that alive. She just had a slight pain in her neck! As my husband was telling me of the accident that she had had and that she was in hospital the Holy Spirit whispered to me reminding me of the time of fasting and praying He had led us to have, to which God has been gracious to me and has answered our prayers. But what if I had been in the world and never heard His voice? He knew what was going to happen and He called me to stand in the place of prayer. As children of God we should pray without ceasing and be ready to hear from God. When He speaks it is for our own good, so we should obey immediately and not procrastinate. I thank God for calling me to pray and giving me the grace to act according to His will. He rescued my daughter from death and saved me from mourning over my child. I will continually sing His praises every day of my life."

As though turning the incident over in my mind, I prompted. "Was the car completely squashed?" She responded, "Completely squashed!" and with a sense of humour added "and now the Mercedes group are using it as an advertisement that it's the strength of their car that protected her – that is to say that the person in the car had no scratches!"

"My fourth testimony concerns myself. Sometime ago whilst I was in London, I started questioning God for not calling me to serve Him when I was younger. He probably did, but I just did not answer! After questioning Him I then said, 'Daddy if only you will reduce my age by ten years, then I can serve you with ten years more so that when I am seventy years of age I will be serving with a strength of sixty years.' About a week later I attended the Holy Ghost service in London where Pastor Adeboye was ministering. During the ministration, a word of knowledge came forth through him that there was a woman in the congregation who wanted God to reduce her age by ten years, so that she could be ten years younger. The Pastor said God had granted her the request. I jumped up praising the Lord and claimed the word as mine."

Looking at her in amazement and with excitement in my voice and in awe of the precision of God's Word through His servant I said, "Exactly what you were telling the Lord!" In a dramatic expression Oluremi Ayida in a loud voice reaffirmed, "Exactly what I was telling the Lord! and I asked, "God! Is that You?" This is my God, He is awesome! Our God is a great God who hears all our requests and grants us the desires of our hearts if it is in line with His will and purposes. It was tailored precisely like that. I hadn't shared with anyone about this. Wasn't that word for me?" Laughing as she spoke, "That is grace!" She concluded saying, "So if I say that I am eighty then I am seventy! I said God make me any age you want!"

Oluremi Ayida joyfully concluded her testimonies adding that there are many more in other areas of her life and ministry that reveal the power of God to establish His will and purposes for her. With the inspired destiny placed in the heart of this *Jewel of God*, many have been reached and are still being reached and blessed in diverse ways through the Gospel of our Lord Jesus Christ. Time and space will not allow for all the wonderful works of God and His thoughts cannot be recounted for they are countless! (Psalm 40:5, Psalm 139: 16-17.)

One should use praise to recognize what one is not.
Elias Canetti

16

HER PRODUCT

You are the light of the world.
A city that is set on a hill cannot be hidden.

Nor do they light a lamp and put it under a basket,
but on a lamp stand,
and it gives light to all who are in the house.

Let your light so shine before men,
that they may see your good works
and glorify your Father in heaven.

Matthew 5:14-16.

While you are enriched in everything for all liberality,
which causes thanksgiving through us to God.
For the administration of this service not only supplies the needs
of the saints, but also is abounding through many thanksgivings
to God, while, through the proof of this ministry, they glorify
God for the obedience of your confession to the gospel of Christ,
and for your liberal sharing with them and all men, and by their
prayer for you, who long for you because of the exceeding grace
of God in you.

2 Corinthians 9:11-14

The account written of the women in the Bible describes their various encounters with JESUS and the corresponding effect it had on their lives, families, communities and nations and the whole world!

… And certain women, who had been healed of evil spirits and
infirmities, Mary called Magdalene, out of whom had come
seven demons, and Joanna the wife of Chuza, Herod's steward
and Susanna, and many others who provided for Him from their
substance.

Luke 8:2-3

The woman then left her waterpot, went her way into the city, and said to the men, "Come and see a Man who told me all things that I ever did. Could this be the Christ?" Then they went out of the city and came to Him. And many of the Samaritans of that city believed in Him because of the word of the woman who testified...
John 4:28-30, 39

At Oluremi Ayida's salvation encounter and experience, the Lord by His Spirit filled her with zeal. She went all out for the Lord in worship, in fellowship and in discipleship as Paul wrote in the fourteenth verse of the ninth chapter of the book of Hebrews.

"...How much more shall the blood of Christ, who through the eternal Spirit, offered Himself without spot to God, purge your conscience from dead works to serve the living God?"

Just as the encounters never left those women as they were, for it was so profound that God used them to affect lives positively and to bring many more lives into His kingdom; so also the life of God's handmaiden, Oluremi Ayida, has the same testimony. It has brought a new song not only into her life but also into her family, work, community, nation and to the Earth! She is sold out for Christ. He is the 'product' she carries and also stands for everywhere she goes, by His abundant grace and ability upon her.

I have known her for more than three decades. She is my senior sister. As children we grew up together. She is very kind, loving, generous, patient, humble and motherly. She is a mother to me; she is there for me any time. She paid for my surgery in the USA in 1997, when I could not walk. She is a wonderful sister to have. I could never have prayed for a better sister in my life. I thank God for putting her in my life.

She is a committed, devoted and dedicated Christian. She can go any length to help those who are in need.

Mrs E. A. Nanna
EDWJ Co-ordinator

I came into the family slightly before they had their first child. Mummy's love, care and open-heartedness, has kept me a member of the family for the past fifty years or so. I lived with them and got all my education from infancy till I graduated in 1976. Living in the home was fun; it definitely gave me privileges I would never have dreamed of, if I had grown up, with my natural parents. Twice I was sponsored on a trip to London, which I considered real extra nice...to be given such opportunities.

For as long as I have known her, the times when she has been nicest, are the Christmas seasons when she will go to all length to make sure everybody feels a part of the family.

Mummy had moral standards she expected her daughters to adhere to. She also trained us to be efficient in cooking, baking, and shopping for the family, which I have found invaluable. She made sure we dressed properly, tidied our rooms, faced our studies, gave correct accounts of our spending, whenever she sent us on a shopping errand. She taught us by example that a woman doesn't fold her hands, but works. As a younger child, it was always better not to overstep your bounds else you will get it! Shouts and scolds when you've done wrong. I was in the habit of burning her soup when cooking, because I would be in the parlour watching T.V. So, I'll be disciplined. She doesn't hide her feelings and now I see that is better because once she has got it out, it's over. Next thing she's relating to you, just as if nothing happened. The first three children I had, she took the trouble to come and visit me in Kaduna where we live which I appreciated immensely. She is always concerned and encouraging us to move ahead in life.

She bought a panel van in 1978 for me and paid for my trip to the USA and Israel in 1987 and 1997 respectively. She has given countless gifts to me and to my family. In the year 2000, our business centre was attacked and she rose up to the task of helping us refurbish it. Mummy is even sweeter now. Before, while we were growing up, I used to be afraid to be too close to her but we relate better now and flow quite well. When I remember all her goodness to my family and me I cannot help blessing her and praying that God will bless her and everything precious in her life. She is a woman of many parts, very approachable and willing to share what God has blessed her with. Her name will definitely go down in history as a great woman!

Mrs Jolomi Owojaiye, (Nee Ayida, sister-in-law)

EDWJ Distributor in Kaduna

I first met Mrs Ayida in 1966. We became very close family friends. I found her to be very caring, humble, hospitable and affable. She is visionary, dedicated, patient, understanding and dependable, competent and open to new ideas in the work of the ministry. I recall that when my husband and I had to move from Government residential quarters upon retirement in 1984, Mrs Ayida took the initiative and offered us and our children accommodation in their home for nearly a year. She readily from the depth of heart empathises with people who are in one difficulty or another and she is ever willing to offer godly counsel and where necessary, offer practical assistance.

Mrs C. A. Omatsone
Administrator, FBFM

I met Mrs Ayida in New York for the very first time over ten years ago. Looking at her I guessed she was a Christian, and after speaking with her I became convinced. I see her as a respectable, intelligent and a God-fearing woman. I discussed a problem with her, immediately, she prayed with me and to the glory of God the answer came. She is very considerate, very loving, very kind, very cheerful and very prayerful. She is a woman of faith, she loves the Lord dearly. She is a prayerful woman and a very considerate boss.

Mrs Owoeye
Counselling Ministry, FBFM

About eighteen years ago, I met Mrs Ayida. I saw her as friendly, zealous, having a heart for God, open, frank and caring. To me she is a leader, a friend and a confidante. When I did not always have transportation to and from the office, anytime Mrs Ayida knows I am in the office she will always call to find out if, I needed a lift back. I found that concern really touching. She is concerned and meticulous. She has a spirit of excellence and she is ready to use talents around her to achieve the goal at hand without embarrassment to her person.

Mrs Nkiru A. Green
FBC Chairperson

I met Mrs Ayida around 1980 when she came to see my mother-in-law whom she knows. As members of the same church she invited me to a Bible Study, for which she came by the house to pick me up for. She is very friendly, cheerful and helpful. When she is talking about the Lord, she gives her all to whatever she is doing. She is Godly, energetic, full of encouraging words, not easily provoked and caring. Mrs Ayida, in order for the work of God to progress would stomach all sorts of rudeness and disrespect from some members. She never loses her cool, she tries all the time to explain things and pacify members; and if they are adamant, she takes it to the Lord in prayers. Watching her relate, has taught us the power of patience and of trusting God to deal with difficult cases. I believe it is because of her relating and caring skill that the ministry is still growing strong. Aunty is a good leader. At all times she shows good example. Nothing is below her to do for the Lord and nothing is too expensive or hard to do for the Lord. I have learnt a lot from watching her. Her zeal for the Lord is great and God is using her mightily. She carries herself elegantly, she works tirelessly and she cares for all members. It's a pleasure and a blessing to know her, work with her and relate with her.

Mrs Victoria Majekodunmi.

Deputy National Co-ordinator, FBFM

On arrival from Ghana in 1994, I met Mrs Oluremi Ayida at a fellowship centre in Victoria Island at the Akinrele's residence. Our level of relationship has being that of a mother to a son. She is a child of God who loves God above all things. She's a great woman of God, courageous and faithful to God's calling. She is compassionate, prayerful, committed, dedicated to duty and generous. There was a time when I needed a loan to get an accommodation. Straight to my surprise it was approved and she also assisted me financially to attend a computer school. She is very committed to God and His work and she is also a down-to-earth woman with special love for her children.

Pastor Joel

FBFM

I met Mrs Ayida in 1982. I have been working with her since then as her driver. She's like a mother to me. She is loving, generous and a Godly mother, so religious. She has changed my life and made me what I am today.

Mr Dickson Amomoh

(Personal Driver)

I first met Mrs Ayida in July 1990 and have a relationship with her as a staff, having being privileged to have worked with all the Administrators of the Ministry to date. The zeal by which she works out things interests me. A particular example was during the children's *holiday camp organised by the ministry. She is hardworking, always ready to spend extra time. She has a desire for the best; a disciple of Christ and a companion at work. The distribution of **Every Day with Jesus**, the planned visits of Rev. Selwyn Hughes to Nigeria have had a great effect on the lives of people and on the ministry. The patience of Mrs Ayida with the staff at different levels is also worthy of mention. She is good and she has made us (Mr Olawale and myself) to be addicted to work. I treasure her words.*

Mr Godwin
Sales & Marketing Staff, FBFM

The first time I met Mrs Ayida was in 1983. Since then, I have had a personal relationship with her. I also relate with her as a Christian mentor. The first impression and perception I had of her was infectious. Her excitement about Christianity and her sense of wonder about God was childlike. Her faith is total. She is tenacious, focused, determined, sympathetic and sincere. There was a time I needed a confidante and she was there with her resilient quietness. She is a good listener, and her solutions to problems are never confrontational. At first, I considered that she was timid and not willing to confront people. I realised later, that she has tremendous respect for people even much younger people like me. This prevents her from being discourteous, or rude. She is always polite and accommodating. One limitation I always wondered about was her anxiety. She is always anxious for things to go well. She plans things in detail, and may duplicate responsibilities, if only to be sure that it gets done.

Bridget Itsueli (Mrs)
Associate & FBC Member

I met Mrs Ayida twelve years ago. She is my MOTHER IN THE LORD. She is a golden example of a woman who loves JESUS. She is humble, gentle, gracious and lovely. She has prophesied so much into my life. The Spirit of God is upon her. God has used her to bless me in many ways that are unknown to her.

Sola Momoh (Mrs)
FBC Member

I first met Mrs Ayida over 10 years ago, may be up to 12-14 years ago, this was when her group invited my husband, Pastor Austen Ukachi as one of the prayer leaders to be involved in prayer mobilisation for the first visit of Selwyn Hughes. I have a relationship with her both at the ministerial and personal level. My first impression and perception of her was, "Here is an elderly woman, a wife, mother and grandmother, well placed in the society, living in one of the best places in the city, married to one of the most prominent men, serving the Lord with vigour, fervency, consistency and so much joy, giving her time to the Lord, why can't I – a woman much younger?" I see her as humble, loving, caring, hardworking, prompt and consistent. One particular note of event involving Mrs Ayida that I will always remember was that once, well over ten years ago, we invited Mama to come and preach during a seminar. She came very simple and challenged us to serve the Lord with gladness. Without any attempt to blow her own trumpet she challenged us with some of the things God led her to do for others for instance the children she gave scholarships to out of her meagre pension as a retired nurse. In our church, a Pastor who recently turned forty years in 2004, testified of how mummy off set his hospital bill after being involved in a ghastly motor accident where he sustained multiple broken bones and most of the other victims died. Mummy never knew the young man, she only read about the case in our prayer bulletin and she sent him money to pay for his hospital bill. When the women's arm of our church, Women Alive gave Mummy an award for faithfulness in Christian service sometimes in year 2004, the young man took permission from the senior Pastor to publicly testify to Mama's kind-heartedness. It was the first time most of us knew about it. While lots of people could not help shedding tears that day, to celebrate the concern, caring nature and sacrifice of a great mother. Not only that, the fact that Mrs Ayida has effectively, efficiently and consistently led the Friendship Bible Fellowship Ministry (FBFM) all these years to greater and greater levels of success is a testimony to her tenacity, industriousness and great leadership skills. No encomium is too much for this truly great and wonderful mother who has given birth to many children for the Lord Jesus Christ and His kingdom. Many women (and men too) started ministry but due to lack of consistency, perseverance e.t.c. were not able to continue; this is not so of Mummy Ayida. We have watched the ministry under her able and most outstanding leadership grow tremendously. There is so much to say. I can go on and on, about Mummy Ayida. As the person through whose ministry God promoted the use of *EveryDay with Jesus*, (A very expository and *inspirational devotional guide) one can only imagine the extent of Mummy's contribution in the spiritual realm. I know colleagues, friends, neighbours, and family members who ordinarily, would not have known how to approach their daily devotion or read the Bible; but who have received help in this area and are now able to read the word of God with perception and understanding through E.D.W.J. For this unique achievement, we thank God for Mrs Ayida and her ministry, the F.B.F.M. Not only that, I was also once in her office to see her, only to learn that she has gone for a visit, (as that was the day in the week when she does her visitation). I exchanged glances with the young Pastor that was with me and we both wondered aloud where a seventy plus year old woman, finds strength to visit on a regular basis. Indeed, from this, one can see that mummy is also a woman of great strength. I have also observed that she takes keen interest in the affairs of all those who are with her in the ministry. She takes time to attend their occasions and rejoices or weeps with them, even when such occasions are not in Lagos. We younger women in ministry, find it difficult to do this, even when such occasions are in Lagos. This makes mummy a leader, a model, a mentor and a great inspiration to our generation. May mummy have many more years of fruitful service, in good health in the vineyard of the Lord. We her children arise and call her blessed. May her tribe increase, may all her children and their generation after them be taught and blessed of the Lord, forever, Amen!*

Pastor (Mrs) Oluyide Ukachi
He's Alive Chapel

*I met Mrs Ayida over fifty years ago when we were both teenagers aspiring to go abroad for further studies. She is very smart, attractive, intelligent, unassuming and very articulate. Mrs Ayida is very religious and her prayer life worth emulating. She will not inconvenience you in any way if you happen to share a bedroom with her. She will wake up very early in the morning, retire to the bathroom to read her bible instead of disturbing you with the lights on. She is always ready to help you any time. She is a good counsellor. She is trustworthy, dependable, selfless and considerate. Mrs Oluremi Ayida is very generous to a fault. She is always willing to help the underprivileged and contributes generously to the work of God. Very committed and responsible, she introduced **Every Day with Jesus** into Nigeria and it is widely read all over the country. She* *performed very well in the Bible College and she is a good leader in the community. She is a good mother and loveable wife.*

Nursing colleague and President of the International Women Society, Lagos

I have known the modest and gracious wife of Mr Allison Ayida – a well-known and highly respected technocrat, for close to four decades.

Our first contact was at a Christian gathering on my return from England and ever since then has constantly and genuinely demonstrated her obedience to the Holy Spirit through many forms of Charitable works intended to promote love, compassion, modesty, integrity, wisdom and faith in God.

Like a loveable mother, she guided and educated me on authentic dignity of the person and of work.

As a courteous woman, she recognises the likeness of God in every soul. Her deep moral foundation no doubt, enables her to recognise the divine imprint in another person.

She impacts true fraternal love on anyone she comes across. The luminous testimony to her compassion is never lacking. Her concern for the common good made me to take intense interest in her virtues.

As a devout born again Christian, her hunger for Christ is visible and is reflected in her increased esteem for the dignity of others and proclamation of the truth of Christ.

She is a woman of wisdom. Her modesty reinforces her gift of discernment and that enables her to manage information with great wisdom.

Her life of prayer is worthy of emulation. She lives the faith as friendship with God and bears the burden (spiritual and material needs) of all her friends.

I have decided to adopt her as my Christian Mother. She stood by me in and out of season and supported me physically, emotionally and spiritually.

She is the real mother in Israel. The Grace of God resides abundantly in her.

It is such a wonderful privilege to share some thoughts about our relationship.

148

God bless you Ma for being a great and inspiring mother. With Affection,

Dr (Mrs) Cecilia Ibru
Associate & FBC Member

The verses in the thirty-first chapter of the book of Proverbs boldly assert that if the virtuous woman will give herself to her God called work, she will be successful in her efforts. There is no equivocating on God's part here. Ultimately He will *"give her of the fruit of her hands, and let her own works praise her in the gates."*

God has used Oluremi Ayida's life as a blessing to so many lives in diverse ways and forms through His blessings, upon her life, to His praise and glory. Her faith, coupled with her works, is well reported of by the families, friends, associates and co-workers in God's vineyard as it was also spoken of concerning Dorcas (Acts 9:36). This is confirmed from God's word as James wrote in his book.

Thus also faith by itself, if it does not have works is dead.
But someone will say, "You have faith and I have works."
Show me your faith without your works,
and I will show you my faith by my works.
James 2:17-18.

What you become is far more important than what you get.
What you get will be influenced by what you become.
Jim Rohn

EPILOGUE

'Every day will be a new experience
until I see my Lord face to face ...'

The above statement by God's handmaiden, Oluremi Ayida could be described as the capstone of her call and walk with God through life's journey. It reveals desire, expectation and a certainty of the ultimate meeting with the Connoisseur of life. God graciously bestows mankind with the gift of life and existence. And in His innermost desire for a living fellowship and relationship with man, He lovingly but sacrificially gave the gift of salvation to mankind through His Son Jesus Christ, the Saviour of the world.

As we journey through life, walking in His revealed grace of life, His purposes and plan unfold and with this comes the ability by His Spirit to walk therein.

Oluremi Ayida since her conversion well over twenty years ago has in her heart a thirst to know more about God and His Word and also to share this knowledge with others through every avenue He makes possible. It burns in her to fulfil divine mandate – a life of not just being successful but much more of a relevant significance. A life that brings positive change and influences many for eternity in God.

She has realised that though she may have many admirers, friends, and family, no one will ever take the place of her Lord. His place in her life is the foundation of every success she will ever have. He has been there in every moment of pain and glory. He is the One that brings her life together. It is His love for her that has kept her mind from breaking under the challenges of life, and when all is said and done there is a part of her life that no one can have but her Lord.

Of a truth indeed, there is a new experience each day. As we seek God to find out His expectations of us from day to day, we will find ourselves released to rejoice in exactly who, what and where we are in Him.

The Apostle Paul in his epistle says he counts himself not to have attained, forgetting the past, he keeps pressing on into each new day with his goals and experience with God for the prize of a high calling in Christ. (Philippians 3: 13-14). He kept fighting a good fight of faith until his course was finished and there was an expectation of receiving a crown of righteousness from His Lord (2 Timothy 4: 7-8).

Ultimately, it is not about the approval and praises of man alone though these carry divine approval as the Bible says: 'Let your light so shine before men, that they may see your good works, and glorify your Father which is in heaven. (Matthew 5: 16). The commendation is finally of God.

Our entire pilgrimage culminates when we are met with the statement:

> *'... Well done, good and faithful servant ...*
> *Enter into the joy of your Master.'*
> *(Matthew 25:21)*

Will it be a translation into an eternal bliss and glory?

God has planted eternity in the human heart (Ecclesiastes 3: 1 1) for there is definitely another life beyond the present. He says if it is in this world alone we have hope in Christ, we are of all men most miserable (1 Corinthians 15: 19). Our hope transcends beyond our earthly sojourn. The ultimate is the truth that: Christ in us, the hope of glory! (Colossians 1: 27).

Whilst we are here fulfilling and accomplishing God's purposes and destiny for us, Christ in our hearts, and living His life through us, reveals God's glory in our lives and gives us an assurance of eternal glory.

The story goes on ...

AFTERWORD

Our great God and Saviour, as we know, is constantly at work orchestrating the affairs of His Kingdom and nothing is more wonderful than the way He allows one life to intersect with another. If ever there was a divine purpose in two people meeting up it was my contact with Remi Ayida. Her first connection with me was as a result of her reading *Every Day with Jesus*. At first it was a low-key situation in the sense that here was an overseas reader, one of many from different parts of the world, writing to me expressing interest in my writings and of wanting to introduce it to her contacts in the Friendship Bible Fellowship Ministries, Nigeria.

Slowly however her requests for copies began to increase to such a degree that I felt that I needed to meet with this energetic and enterprising woman who seemed to have such a strong influence in the nation of Nigeria. When eventually we did meet I realised that I was standing in the presence of a very unique and remarkable person. Her dedication and commitment to Christ simply oozed through her personality and her desire to help people get into the Bible on a regular basis warmed my heart for that too is what I have committed my whole life to – helping people develop an appetite for the Scriptures.

Over the course of time (now getting close to twenty years) Remi's many qualities have come to the fore in the sense that she had co-ordinated the printing and distribution of *Every Day with Jesus* in Nigeria, to the point where Nigeria now has the largest readership of any country in the world! In addition to this she has co-ordinated a number of visits of myself and my team to Nigeria – Lagos, Owerri, Port Harcourt and Abuja where I and the members of my team have ministered to large crowds.

One of the things that has impressed me about Remi is the fact that she has the ear of so many influential persons in the nation of Nigeria. I have seen bishops and politicians stand respectfully in her presence and as I have watched I have seen by the expressions on their faces a certain admiration for the work she does and accomplishes for Jesus Christ.

She appears also content to remain in the background and let others take the credit for the projects she has initiated – a true characteristic of someone who is secure enough in her relationship with Jesus Christ to seek neither the applauds or the glory.

Remi is one of the jewels in God's timepiece of redemption and I am glad that I can own her as one of my best and dearest friends.

Rev. Dr. Selwyn Hughes.
Founder, Crusade for World Revival (CWR)
And Author of *Every Day with Jesus* (EDWJ)

APPENDIX

Individual Reviews of *Jewel of God*

It is a great privilege for me to write a review of the biography of the one I respectfully call "Sisi Remi".

Ever since I met Mrs Oluremi Ayida in the mid-sixties of the twentieth century, I have remained highly impressed, indeed enthused, by her love, kindness, generosity, gentle nature, respect and regard for both high and low, humility, tolerance, spirit of encouragement, consideration for people generally and her ability to see something good in every individual.

The biography of Mrs Oluremi Ayida, the handmaid of God as the title *Jewel of God*, depicts is most welcome and timely, having regard to the fact that happenings worldwide underscore the need for people to draw close to God.

Indeed Mrs Oluremi Ayida's hard work, her relentless effort, her devotion to the Lord, her commitment to whatever course the Lord leads her to take, her generousity in giving to the work of God, and her ability to manage skilfully both human and material resources have made her truly a Jewel of God.

It is desirable to mention that Mrs Oluremi Ayida even at her local church which is also mine, Our Saviour's Church, TBS, Lagos, in her own quiet, gentle, but effective and affective way has worked for the transformation of lives. She was at the first meeting of the Bible Study Fellowship, the first Ministry in the Parish Church, she initiated the Prayer Fellowship and the Counselling Ministry with emphasis on marriage counselling. These ministries have helped in no small way to make Christianity not a Sunday Sunday medicine, but a way of daily living. Indeed the Ayida couple is held in high esteem in the Church. The way she also relates with Church leaders of other denominations in her desire and effort at promoting and transforming lives in homes and community makes one see the Lord's prayer that all believers be one being fulfilled in her.

Without the least hesitation, I would say that the biography of Mrs Oluremi Ayida herein presented is a testimony to the fact that the only life worth living is the life in Christ, a life directed and controlled by the Holy Spirit, a life of service to God and to humanity, a life in which one is dead to oneself, but alive to Christ. It is a life which gives honour and glory to the Lord God and blessing to others. Such a life is bound to have challenges, trials and tribulations. However, with Christ victory is sure. Such is the life of Mrs Oluremi Ayida.

That this is Mrs Oluremi Ayida's life is strongly and vividly attested to by great Church leaders like Pastor E.A. Adeboye of the Redemed Christian Church of God and Revd Dr Selwyn Hughes before he passed on to the great beyond, the family members of Mrs Oluremi Ayida, and some of the prominent and fervent members of FBC whose lives Mrs Oluremi Ayida has imparted on greatly.

Mrs Oluremi Ayida had prayed that the history of her life be written. The Lord answered this in using Sope Macarthy-Chiadika, to do a good job of getting Mrs Oluremi Ayida to herself tell her story while she the author interjects with relevant and appropriate passages from the Scriptures, Christian literature and by world Christian leaders thereby highlighting the scriptural basis of the whole work.

One sees from this approach that both the subject of the biography and the author are daughters of the living God.

Mrs Oluremi Ayida's desire to have her biography produced has only one singular purpose, which is, the promotion and extension of God's Kingdom here on earth. She believes it should encourage people to surrender their lives to God through studying His word and praying without ceasing. This is in line with her ministry – The ministry of WORD AND PRAYER.

It is a biography that would lead to conversion and also deepen the faith of believers. Consequently, it is one to honour and glorify God. It is my fervent desire that all readers be challenged by the story herein told to strive individually to become "One of the Jewels in God's Time Piece of Redemption."

God bless you all as you read. Amen.

Jane O. Ejueyitchie-Oroye (Mrs)
Educationist; (Former Principal of Queens College,
Yaba, Lagos).

An extremely interesting and inspiring biography ... In *Jewel of God* Sope Macarthy-Chiadika presents a vivid and fascinating account of the life of a truly remarkable woman, Remi Ayida. Viewed from 16 different angles, Remi is indeed 'a life full of God, faithfulness, excitement and a great example worthy of emulation.' In seeking to honour her, Sope has nevertheless succeeded in holding God at the centre of the story, as the source and inspiration of all that Remi has achieved, not least as founder of the Friendship Bible Fellowship Ministries and ministry partner to CWR in Nigeria.

My own acquaintance with Remi began in the early 1990s when she introduced *Every Day with Jesus* to a Nigerian readership. From the first 100 copies she took back from the UK to her friends in Nigeria, she built up a readership of hundreds of thousands, so that today Nigeria has, by far, more readers of this devotional than any other country in the world. Remi and the FBFM committee she formed also organised many CWR ministry visits to Nigeria over the years and enabled us to share with Nigerians from all walks of life the heart of our Bible teaching. Throughout the years of our association she has revealed herself as a woman of outstanding integrity in a world where, sadly, corruption is common place.

Although I felt I knew Remi well, and had visited her in her home in Nigeria, there was much to learn of her history and I have loved reading about her early years, her job, her courtship and marriage and her family and extended family life. I found myself captivated by the story Sope tells and thrilled by the revelation of God's work in Remi's life. I know that many readers will eagerly turn the pages of this book, as I did, and be delighted to encounter there the woman I have come to admire, deeply respect and love.

Jeannette Barwick
Head of Special Ministries
CWR, Waverley Abbey House,
Farnham, Surrey, England

Jewel of God – A Christian bestseller – this is a must read for all believers and non-believers alike! The person of Mama Ayida brings to life – to the glory of God, a heart that loves God, patiently trusts God, serves God and is blessed and empowered of God! Through the reading of this book, which brings to light a great life in Christ, I have come to see 2 Corinthians 10: 5-7 and Romans 8: 28 as new revelations! I particularly recommend this book for all leaders in the body of Christ and trustworthy ministers of the Gospel – it will inspire, challenge and build you to fulfilling your purpose in Christ – only through His Spirit!

Victor Macarthy
Pastor, Christ Harvest Centre, Edmonton, London
An Elim Pentecostal Church